Another Look
At The Parables Of Jesus

Stories
To
Remember

Ron Lavin

CSS Publishing Company, Inc., Lima, Ohio

STORIES TO REMEMBER

Copyright © 2002 by
CSS Publishing Company, Inc.
Lima, Ohio

Unless otherwise marked, Scripture quotations are taken from the *Holy Bible, New International Version*. Copyright © 1973, 1978, 1984 International Bible Society. Used by permission of Zondervan Bible Publishers. All rights reserved.

Scripture quotations marked (RSV) are from the *Revised Standard Version of the Bible*, copyrighted 1946, 1952 ©, 1971, 1973, by the Division of Christian Education of the National Council of the Churches of Christ in the USA. Used by permission.

Scripture quotations marked (KJV) are from the *King James Version of the Bible*, in the public domain.

Library of Congress Cataloging-in-Publication Data

Lavin, Ronald J.
   Stories to remember : another look at the parables of Jesus / Ron Lavin.
    p. cm.
   ISBN 0-7880-1891-4 (pbk. : alk. paper)
   1. Jesus Christ—Parables. I. Title.
   BT377 .L38 2002
   226.8'.06—dc21   ·   2002004184

For more information about CSS Publishing Company resources, visit our website at www.csspub.com or e-mail us at custserv@csspub.com or call (800) 241-4056.

ISBN 0-7880-1891-4   PRINTED IN U.S.A.

This book is dedicated to

- *Merle Franke and George Hoog, my mission supervisors when I came out of seminary in 1960 and worked in a garage church in Lebanon, Indiana*

- *Mission pastor Abbey Byrd, pastor of Good Shepherd Lutheran Church in Alpine, California, and all mission pastors throughout the country*

- *Dr. Mel Keischnick, adult study leader at Calvary Lutheran Church in Solana Beach, California, and all the leaders of adult study groups and classes in our churches*

- *Rod Anderson and Bud Potter, who set an example of lay ministry at King of Glory Lutheran Church in Fountain Valley, California. Bud started* Go And Do Likewise. *Rod is a congregational leader like the best "church elders" of the past. He also works with* Go And Do Likewise

- *Stan Beard and Maury Skones and all Directors of Music in our churches, who tell Bible stories in memorable church music, and*

- *Joyce, my wife, and our daughters, Dell, Diane, and Mary, and their families, who share with me in the wonderful tradition of storytelling around the kitchen table.*

Books By Ron Lavin

The *Another Look* Series
I Believe; Help My Unbelief: Another Look At The Apostles' Creed
Stories To Remember: Another Look At The Parables Of Jesus

To be published soon:
Abba: Another Look At The Lord's Prayer
The Big Ten: Another Look At The Ten Commandments
Saving Grace: Another Look At The Sacraments

Other Books In Print
Turning Griping Into Gratitude
Empty Spaces; Empty Places (written with Constance Sorenson)
Way To Grow!
The Advocate
The Great I AM
Previews Of Coming Attractions

Previously Published Books
Alone / Together
You Can't Start A Car With A Cross
You Can Grow In A Small Group
Jesus In Stained Glass
Jesus Christ, The Liberator (written with Bill Grimmer, MD)
Hey, Mom, Look At Me!

Table Of Contents

Foreword

by Merle G. Franke
Former Lutheran Church In America
Secretary for Church Development

My acquaintance with Ron Lavin goes back to his graduation from college and has continued through the years of his ministry. Lavin's experience as a parish pastor, evangelism specialist, renowned preacher, and prolific author would be more than sufficient to recommend this latest book. In addition, his personal faith and biblical-based preaching equip him well to lead us through a collection of sixteen parables of Jesus.

In his introduction, Lavin states that Jesus' parables invite us into a new world — the kingdom of God. The term itself, he notes, is a coded term. But far from abandoning the term, Lavin urges that we keep it because it was obiously important and significant to Jesus, who used parables to assist his listeners to understand and cherish the term. Lavin further de-codes "kingdom of God" through his explanation of the parables, bringing them more easily into the twenty-first century. He uses the helpful analogy of parables being like "snapshots" to help Bible readers understand the point of parables. He points out what should be obvious to modern readers, but which we often overlook, i.e., that Jesus used illustrations in his parables that were common to the average householder in his day, but which might sound strange to us.

Lavin has a way of peeling off the layers of a parable's intent to bring the reader directly to the point. An example is found in chapter two, the parable of the Good Samaritan. The main point of the story, he points out, is not necessarily that we should be good to those in need — important as that is — but rather the importance of putting our faith into *action*. The lawyer in the parable is more interested in a philosophical discussion of "neighbor" than he is in putting his faith into action.

It is this kind of interpretation and assistance that will lead readers of this book to delve more deeply into the impact the parables can have on their own actions. Lavin doesn't leave that to chance. At the end of each chapter are questions for group discussion and/or personal consideration. Also a section in the back of the book titled Digging Deeper encourages readers to further discussion of the parables. Thus the book lends itself to small group Bible study, Sunday school classes, and the like.

The parables of Jesus as presented in Scripture will always be a deep well of meaning for those who study the Bible. In this book Ron Lavin helps us to drink from that well.

Merle G. Franke is the author of *In Other Words* (a book on the parables of Jesus).

Introduction

Stories To Remember is a book on the parables of Jesus intended for personal inspiration and devotions, for small groups of Christians meeting in homes, for Sunday school classes and for pastors who preach on the parables. The parables of Jesus have inspired me; I hope this book will help these parables come alive for you, the reader.

The stories of Jesus often intrigue us, challenge us, and cause us to remember Jesus. These stories remember Jesus for us. In the parables, the storyteller comes rushing into the present from the past as we hear or read what he said. In the Bible, remembrance means participation. Remembrance means actualizing the past.

The stories of Jesus invite us into a new world called the kingdom of God. A shift from our world to the world of Jesus can take place as we hear or read the stories Jesus told. The kingdom of God is so important that I venture to say that it is the most important concept in the Bible, but there is a problem with it. The kingdom of God is a coded, religious, and technical term.

Technical terms drive us mad. They contain code words that are often misunderstood. Lawyers and medical doctors use code words. Insurance companies have them. Intellectuals, universities, and educators love to use technical terms. Government agencies like the Internal Revenue Service and Social Security Administration are the worst offenders! Sometimes I think that some of the people who use all this technical language don't understand their own code words. They use them to confuse us. Why can't we just use plain words of one syllable that people understand?

I'm a fairly intelligent guy. Don't try to snow me or impress me with long complicated concepts. Say what you mean. I will say what I mean. We can communicate! But no, people and institutions use big, long words with hidden meaning that only the enlightened can understand.

"Yes, Ron," someone is saying, "but you religious leaders are guilty of the same confusion. Homiletics and hermeneutics, eschatological and anthropological — these are all technical terms with long tails. Speak plainly so that we understand what you are saying. The kingdom of God is one of these mystical terms that the average person cannot understand." My excuse for retaining the term "kingdom of God" is that Jesus used it. He must have had a good reason.

Jesus usually cut through the multiple layers of complex terms. He used simple words of one syllable that simple people could understand. That was his genius. Why then did he retain the term "kingdom of God"? The common people of his time were confused by it. Even the apostles thought that Jesus was talking about a political overthrow of the Roman kingdom when he talked about the kingdom of God.

The truth is that I don't know why Jesus retained the term. Maybe it was because he wanted to invite us into another world, another way of thinking so different from our natural way that we must venture into a new realm to discover it. Maybe he wanted to be sure that his message was consistent with the Old Testament which often uses the term "Day of the Lord's coming," a parallel phrase for the kingdom of God. Maybe he wanted us to stretch and learn something new. Maybe he saw the concepts of King, Lord, or ruler as the keys to understanding all of his teaching. Whatever the reason, Jesus used the term "kingdom of God" frequently, especially in the parables.

Before we look at the parables themselves, let's look further at the code words that come before many of the parables: "The kingdom of God is like...." Let's look at three dynamic principles of the kingdom of God, a working explanation of the kingdom of God, and an outline of the Bible based on the kingdom of God.

The first dynamic principle is that Jesus never defines the kingdom of God. But then, Jesus never defines God, heaven, or morality either. Jesus illustrates all of these, but he never gives definitions of them. Instead, he tells stories. Jesus is descriptive, not definitive. The whole Bible is that way. Jesus was a Jew. The whole Bible, written by Jews, is descriptive, not giving us narrow definitions, but open-ended stories. Stories give space for us to consider God's grace.

A second dynamic principle for understanding the kingdom of God is that its time frame is explained in a paradoxical way. Jesus talks of the kingdom as both here and coming in the hereafter. He uses both present tense and future tense to describe it. The kingdom of God is coming at some unknown date in the future, but somehow we are supposed to start acting as if it has already come. The kingdom has not come in its fullness. That will come on the "Day of the Lord," at the end of time. Jesus and his parables are previews of coming attractions. They are deposits. They give us a foretaste of things to come.

A third dynamic principle helps us understand end-time coming of the kingdom of God in the light of the present coming of the kingdom. The third principle of the kingdom of God is that the first coming is like lightning; the ultimate coming like thunder. When I was a boy, my mother told me, "Ron, when you see the lightning, you know that the thunder is coming. Count the seconds between the lightning and the thunder and you will know how many miles you are from the lightning." I don't know if my mother was right about the miles, but I am sure that she was right that it would only be a little time before the sound of thunder would follow the sight of lightning.

Likewise, the kingdom of God is coming soon. It may be seconds, minutes, hours, days, decades, or centuries away, but it is coming. We are expected to live on tip-toe, acting on the fact that we live between the lightning and the thunder. Just as surely as the thunder follows the lightning, the second coming of Christ in glory will follow the first coming of Christ in the flesh. The parables of the kingdom are part of the lightning strike of God to let us know what is happening now in the light of what is coming soon.

The three dynamic principles for understanding ultimate truth about the kingdom of God are:

1. Look for descriptive stories rather than definitive thinking.
2. Look for a future and present time frame for the kingdom of God.
3. Look for opportunities to act as if you are living between the lightning and the thunder.

Where do we go from here? Let's consider a working explanation of the meaning of the kingdom of God. A working explanation is less narrow than a limiting definition. It can be broad enough to allow for a paradoxical time frame of future and present and stimulating enough to allow for the high anticipation of living between the lightning and the thunder. Simply put, the best working explanation of the kingdom of God I find in the Bible is the Lordship of God.

The working principle in this book is that the *kingdom of God is God's rule over us for our own good.* The question is not whether or not we will be ruled, but who or what will rule us. An anonymous writer put it this way:

> *Unless that which is above us*
> *Controls that which is within us*
> *That which is around us*
> *Will.*

For our own good, God is the Lord of our lives. That is what the kingdom of God is all about. The first creed of Christianity is "Jesus is Lord." That means that I am called to submit my life to him as my ruler. We are below him, underneath him. One of the meanings of the word "understand" is "to stand under." Only as we stand under Jesus do we understand him. That is what the kingdom of God is all about.

We are subjects. God is king. We are students. God is teacher. We are children. God is Father. Father knows best. We as children often do not know what is best for us. That God is Lord means that he knows what is best for us and has our best interest in mind as he shows us what to do. That is what the kingdom of God is all about. That is what the parables of the kingdom are all about.

A simple three-point outline of the Bible with the kingdom of God as the organizing principle might look something like this. In chapters one and two of Genesis, we discover that Creator God is Lord. He sets the freedom and limits for Adam and Eve. "The one thing to be avoided is the fruit of this one tree," the Lord says.

In chapter three of Genesis we learn that man and woman choose to disobey the order of the Lord. They eat the forbidden fruit. That is disobedience. That is sin.

12

The rest of the Bible, from Genesis 4 through Revelation, is about God offering boundless opportunities to his two-footed handiwork to return to peace and fulfillment through repentance and obedience. Today we live in this third phase. God is still offering unending opportunities for us to return to the state of peace and fulfillment through forgiveness.

The stories of Jesus intersect our lives, giving us numerous opportunities to return to God. "I want you to be in my kingdom," the Lord is saying. "Listen to these stories. They give you open doors to experience now the glory of the kingdom which is coming. They are a call to remember your way home."

Stories To Remember is intended to assist people with their journey home to God. My hope is that it will mostly be used by adult classes and small groups meeting in homes or churches. My experience is that these groups and classes are the most likely setting to wake us up to the realities of God and his kingdom.

The chapters of *Stories To Remember* are divided into two sections for easier handling by these groups and classes. It is easier to take on eight meetings at a time, rather than face sixteen meetings all at once. Points To Ponder are included after each chapter, to look more specifically at the text, its setting and character, in order to better understand it. Questions at the end of each chapter are intended to stimulate discussion.

At the end of the book you will find Tips For Small Group Leaders to assist group leaders in some of the basic practical principles of how small groups work. For further information about small groups, see my book, *Way To Grow! Church Growth Through Small Groups* (CSS Publishing Co., Lima, Ohio, 1998).

In addition, a section called Digging Deeper is intended to help those who choose to do so to go deeper in both spirituality and action as a result of each parable. While no one can design spirituality or an action plan for another, it is my hope that this material will assist readers in both of these areas.

The six parables in Matthew 13:31-33 and 13:44-52 were chosen for the opening chapter in this book, because they are like snapshots of the kingdom of God. All the parables of Jesus might be considered snapshots that help us understand what happened in

13

Jesus' day and interpret what is happening today. As we look back on the parable snapshots of Jesus, we can remember him and apply his messages to our lives today.

Special thanks go to Ruth Hancock and Kathy Shutt who originally typed these chapters, and to Merle Franke, who wrote the Foreword and made suggestions about the content. Tom Lentz, my faithful editor at CSS Publishing Company, helped clarify these chapters. If an idea is clear, it is likely that one of these secretaries or proofreaders helped clarify it. If an idea is not clear, I take full responsibility for it.

Credit for the Points To Ponder and the Digging Deeper sections of this book goes to Tom Lentz who suggested them. Tom's insight that these sections would enrich the study of the parables was right on the mark.

I hope that *Stories To Remember* will be as beneficial to you as a reader as it was productive for me as a writer, preacher, and speaker.

> *There are stories that cannot be silenced.*
> *There are stories that are stronger than death.*
> *There are stories that can raise us from our sins.*
> — *Marty Haugen*

The parables of Jesus are such stories. These stories invite us into a new world called *the kingdom of God* where we live between the lightning (Jesus' first coming) and the thunder (Jesus' second coming). The stories of Jesus intrigue us, challenge us, give us space for grace, and cause us to remember Jesus. They are *Stories To Remember*.

These stories pop our preconceptions and misconceptions, upset our equilibrium, and yet comfort us. The parables are not moral example stories, but warnings and invitations about the illusions that trap us in dark corners where there seems to be no hope left. They are wake-up calls. Each parable is like a bucket of cold water thrown in our face.

You are invited to take another look at the *Stories To Remember*.

Ron Lavin
Encinitas, CA

Books In The "Another Look" Series

Stories To Remember is the second book in the "Another Look" series. The first book, *I Believe; Help My Unbelief* (about the Apostles' Creed) was published by CSS Publishing Company in 2001. The third book, *Abba* (about the Lord's Prayer), the fourth book, *The Big Ten* (about the Ten Commandments), and the fifth book, *Saving Grace* (about the sacraments), will be published between 2002 and 2005.

All of the books in this series are intended for group study as well as individual inspiration. Membership classes, confirmation classes, Bible studies, and koinonia (fellowship) groups will all find these materials helpful for their journey into a deeper faith in God and more consecrated actions for God.

There are two major movements in Christian churches today. One is lay ministry development. The second is the small group movement. The books in the "Another Look" series are intended to assist both of these major growth movements. Specifically, in *Stories To Remember*, the Points To Ponder and the Question sections at the end of each chapter and the Digging Deeper section at the end of this book should help readers move from just considering ideas to being inspired to ministry in action.

For example, a men's group at King of Glory Lutheran Church in Fountain Valley, California, moved from studying about the parable of the Good Samaritan to forming an action group called Go And Do Likewise. This group trims trees, cuts lawns, plants flowers, and paints houses free for the elderly and others who cannot afford to pay someone to do this work. Labor and supplies are free for persons in need. Costs are paid through voluntary contributions of church members who believe in this ministry of service. I was the pastor at King of Glory when this ministry began, but I am proud to announce that I did not start it. Lay people started it. Go And Do Likewise is an excellent example of a group of dedicated lay people putting faith into action by studying a parable and then doing something about it. Putting faith into action by loving service is one of the basic tenets of Christianity.

The books in the "Another Look" series are not only an attempt to get back to the basics of Christianity, but also to go forward with those basics. Many churches today are so caught up with modernity that they have forgotten the foundations of our faith. It is necessary to interpret and apply Christianity to the modern world; it is equally important to invite people today to get into the world of the Bible. The world of the Bible is called the kingdom of God. All of the books in the "Another Look" series deal with the kingdom of God in one way or another. This book is about Jesus' stories about the kingdom.

Section One:

Kingdom Warnings

Chapter One

Six Snapshots

Matthew 13:31-33, 44-52

Have you ever taken snapshots on a vacation trip? Have you ever taken photos of your family and friends or pictures of your new house or car or boat? Have you ever put any or all of these pictures in a photo album and then looked back on them later and remembered the people, places, and events in the photos? Most of us have done these things many times.

That is what we are going to do as we look at the parables of the kingdom of God in the thirteenth chapter of the Gospel of Matthew. We are going to look at six snapshots. These snapshots are not of the Grand Canyon or Grandma and Grandpa; not of the big fish we caught in Minnesota or the big person who used to be a baby; not of the mountains, lakes, and rivers we saw on the last vacation trip we took — no, not any of these, but six snapshots of the kingdom of God as Jesus describes it.

Before we look at these six snapshots, we need to understand that the subject of all of them is the kingdom of God. In the Gospel of Matthew, the term "kingdom of heaven" is used, but it means the same thing: God's rule over us for our own good. The kingdom of God is like a mustard seed, yeast hidden in flour, hidden treasure, a merchant searching for a pearl of great price, a net to catch fish, and students who respect and follow old traditions and venture into new teachings.

A Mustard Seed
Snapshot number one. Click. The kingdom is like a mustard seed (Matthew 13:31-32). The mustard seed is hard to see, so small

that you can hardly detect it, but like the bush or tree which can come from a mustard seed in Israel, it can eventually house the birds of the air.

The motley group of nobodies who first heard these words found it hard to believe that they were the mustard seeds from which great growth would come. A handful of ex-prostitutes, ex-tax collectors, and ex-fishermen hardly make good prospects for turning the world upside down. They didn't know what they were doing. "Just follow my lead," Jesus is saying. The little band of nobodies would become an invincible force for good. That is how it is in the kingdom of God. You do not need to be good or strong. You just have to be under the orders of the One who knows what he is doing. That is what the kingdom of God is like.

Yeast In Flour

Click. Snapshot number two. The kingdom of God is like yeast hidden in three measures of flour (Matthew 13:33). This imagery comes from the kitchen of a Jewish home of Jesus' day. It is common, simple, and practical.

The leaven in ancient Israel was a little piece of leftover dough from a previous baking. It has fermented in the time between the last baking and this one. It has the power to transform the dough. Unleavened bread is flat and unappetizing. Add a little yeast and, wonder of wonders, you have something that after baking becomes soft, porous, and tasty, something that gives off one of the best aromas in the world, freshly baked bread. The kingdom of God is better than freshly baked bread. It is good!

Jesus is saying, "If you submit to the rule of God, you will be like the yeast that causes the dough to rise. It may be little and hidden, but it is powerful as it quietly does its work of causing people to rise."

Hidden Treasure

Snapshot number three. Click. The kingdom of God is like a hidden treasure in the field (Matthew 13:44). Wouldn't you sell everything you have and buy this field? The treasure is beyond your imagination. You will be rich beyond your dreams, not rich in materials or money, but spiritually rich. Sell whatever so-called valuables you have, but don't miss an opportunity to buy this hidden treasure. In the end your material goods will all be trash anyway. Don't miss an opportunity to acquire what Jesus is offering you — in this life the power and presence of God on your side against any and all obstacles and after you die eternal life with our Father.

In this snapshot we see the picture of any sacrifice necessary being made gladly because the kingdom is so much greater than all of our valuables. Only a fool would believe the labels which people have put on the items in the store windows of life today. The cheap things have high prices. The expensive things have low prices. Cars and boats and houses and bank accounts and all material things have been given high price tags. Prayer and church and Christian fellowship and ethical values have all been given low price tags. Only a fool would believe the nonsense of the switched labels.

Look. See things as they really are. Don't swallow the illusions of the Deceiver and his followers. God has the real treasures. They may be hidden, but faith will help you see things the way things really are. We have to take this snapshot out and look at it from time to time to remind ourselves where the real treasures of life are to be found.

The Merchant And The Pearl Of Great Price
Click. Snapshot number four. The kingdom of God is like a merchant in search of the one-of-a-kind pearl of great price (Matthew 13:45-46). Pearls in the ancient world generally came from the shores of the Red Sea or far-off Britain. If you were a woman in Jerusalem in Jesus' time and you had an expensive pearl, you would be the envy of everyone. In your hand or around your neck you would have a thing of surpassing asthetic beauty, the loveliest of possessions. The kingdom of God is better than a lovely, beautiful, and valuable large pearl.

Search for it, my friends. Search for it. It is worth the effort. When you find it, you will be amazed. It will come to you as a gift from your benevolent Father. It is valuable beyond measure, but it

21

will cost you nothing. It is free. Think about it. That is what it is like in the kingdom of God.

To be under God's rule means that you are the owner of a pearl of great price.

A Fisherman Pulling In A Net Full Of Fish

Click. The fifth snapshot is a picture of a fisherman pulling in a net of fish to shore (Matthew 13:47-50). Look at the picture and think about the kingdom of God.

There were two kinds of fishing nets in ancient Israel. One was a casting net thrown out from shore. It had a bell-like top with a long cord attached to the arm of a fisherman. This is not the net that Jesus had in mind when he told this parable.

The second net was used from a boat to drag the waters and the bottom of the Sea of Galilee. This drag net is the one that Jesus had in mind as he told this story. This one forms a great cone. When the net is full, the fishermen in the boat drag it throught the water toward shore. The fishermen jump out of the boat into shallow waters and drag the net up on land.

It is the nature of a drag net that it does not, and cannot, discriminate. All kinds of things get caught in a drag net — both good and bad. A mixture of good and bad, useful and useless items, are brought to shore. Jesus is saying, "It will be your job to catch as many people for the kingdom as you can. You will not be able to discern and absolutely judge who is good and who is bad. Leave that to me. The time of judgment is coming. I will separate the good from the bad when the net gets to shore."

When you are fishers of people, you will know the joy of helping others find their place in the kingdom of God, just as you have found it.

The Old And New Treasure

Click. Number six. Take out this picture and look at it often. It is a picture of scribes and their master looking at old and new treasure (Matthew 13:51-52). A scribe in Jesus' day was someone who wrote down and followed what his master said. He was a student of a wise and successful teacher. The followers of Jesus must write down and learn to do what Jesus did. Jesus, the master of the house, brought out his treasure and displayed it, both old and new treasure.

The old is our heritage, our background, the good teachings we learned as children. The old is the patriarchs and the law and the prophets. The old is the Old Testament. The master takes it out, looks at it, and says, "This is very good."

The new treasure is what Jesus taught us over and above our personal heritage and what the Old Testament says. This is the new teaching we have never heard before. This is the New Testament. Our past knowledge of God and what is good is further extended by the coming of Jesus Christ into our lives. Whatever we bring to the experience of becoming a Christian is enriched and extended by the Lord. Before believing in Christ we were not totally empty, but neither were we full. We were not totally broke, but neither were we rich. Before Christ entered our lives, we were not dead, but we were sick unto death. Christ gives us the gifts of fullness (called maturity), riches (called blessings), and health (called wholeness).

When we come into the kingdom and place our faith in God through Jesus Christ, we receive treasures we can hardly imagine and do not deserve. The old treasures are better than they ever appeared to be. The new treasures are beyond measure.

Maybe someone is saying in his or her heart, "Ron, is all of this really true?" Yes, as far as I know, everything I have told you is based on the Bible, God's revealed Word. The kingdom of God is like a small mustard seed; yeast in a loaf of bread; treasure hidden in a field, just ready for you to discover it; a pearl of great price worth more than all you have; a drag net which catches many different kinds of fish; and like a master and his students who value both the old and new treasure. Every time we share from the Word of God, we must ask, "Is it true?"

But there is another question that must be faced every time we encounter the Word of God. Does it make a difference? Does this passage of Scripture about six pictures of the kingdom of God make a difference in your life? Look at the snapshots and ask, "What difference do they make in my life?"

Points To Ponder

1. *The mustard plant* of Palestine was very different from the mustard plant we know. The tiny grain of mustard seed in Palestine grew into something very like a large bush or tree. The kingdom of heaven starts small, but no one knows how large it may grow or how many birds will nest in it. See Matthew 17:20 where Jesus speaks of faith as small as a grain of mustard seed doing great things.

2. *Leaven (or yeast)* was a little dough left from the last baking. It was part of the everyday experience of Jewish life to see dough rising and then being baked. Jesus' hearers all knew the power of a little leaven in the dough.

   Sometimes leaven was used as an illustration of how a little evil could bring great evil to all around it. See Matthew 16:6, 1 Corinthians 5:6-8, and Galatians 5:9. Here Jesus uses leaven in a positive way to show that a little faith can transform everything around it in a wonderful way.

3. *Hidden treasure* buried in the ground was familiar to common people in Palestine who did not use banks. If a person discovered treasure in a field, he found a precious thing, worth any sacrifice necessary to buy the field in which the treasure was found.

4. *The pearl of great price* was both valuable and beautiful. To find a pearl like this was well worth the difficult search. To find the kingdom of heaven is not a grim duty, but a great joy, exceeding all the other joys of life.

5. *The drag net* in Jesus' story was an illustration that fishermen would easily understand. Since fish were such an integral part of everyday life, most of Jesus' hearers would have understood the way fish were caught in the Sea of Galilee. They would understand that a drag net brought in a mixture of both good and bad fish. As the drag net did not discriminate between the

good and the bad, so we too are not to make judgments about who is good and evil. It is not right for us to judge who is a true Christian and who is not. That judgment belongs to God on judgment day.

6. *The old and new treasures* Jesus speaks of here are the law and the prophets on the one hand and the new treasures he gives his scribes on the other. The old teachings are not eliminated, but illuminated and enlarged by the new teachings Jesus gives. Every new believer comes to faith in Jesus Christ with some gift. The new believer is asked to retain that gift, but enlarge it by the new discovery of faith in Jesus Christ as Lord and Savior.

Questions For Personal Consideration And/Or Group Discussion

1. What are your favorite snapshots?

2. Why do you like them so much?

3. In what ways are the snapshots in the six parables of Jesus like yours?

4. In what ways are these parable snapshots unlike yours?

5. In what ways do these parables make a difference for you?

6. What warnings did you discover in these six parables?

See **Digging Deeper**, p. 157, for further insights and applications.

Chapter Two

Six Questions

Luke 10:25-37

At first glance, the focus of this parable appears to be a generous humanitarian we call the Good Samaritan. The actual focus of this story is a smart but foolish religious lawyer who meets his match and then some in the encounter described in Luke 10:25-37. There is a basic question we must answer right at the beginning, as we examine this parable.

The First Question: Is This Story About Humanism?

In Jesus' parable, there is a stranger by the side of the road who had been attacked by robbers. The man who helped him is called "the good Samaritan." We call good people who help others "good Samaritans." Is the heart of Jesus' parable that we should do acts of kindness? As important as that is, I don't think that this is the heart of the story. Before I tell you why I think that humanism is not the heart of Jesus' parable of the good Samaritan, we should look at the historical background of the Samaritans.

The Samaritans were a crossbreed of Jews and Gentiles, resulting from the residue effect of the Babylonians conquering the Jews in 587 B.C. On that date, Nebuchadnezzar, the Babylonian conqueror-king, captured Jerusalem, destroyed the Temple, and deported the Jews to Babylon to prevent uprisings against his domination. The Babylonians left the poor, the weak, and the nobodies, as a residue. For about fifty years this residue of Jews did what they thought they had to do to survive. They intermarried with neighboring peoples and adapted to the religious and cultural ways of the Gentiles around them. Thus they became a half-breed race called the Samaritans.

When the Jews were allowed to return from Babylon, they rebuilt their city and their Temple under the leadership of Ezra the prophet and Nehemiah the governor. Ezra and Nehemiah tried to restore worship of the one true God and national pride. The returning Jews denounced the Samaritans who had compromised the faith and national pride. This policy was so severe that the Jews of Jesus' time did not even walk through Samaria, the territory of the Samaritans. Instead, when they walked from Judah (the southern kingdom) to Israel (the northern kingdom) and vice-versa, they walked hours out of their way to avoid Samaria.

Jesus used a Samaritan as the hero of the story and two religious leaders, a priest and a Levite, as villains because he wanted the Jews to be open to the possibility that anyone of any background could return to God. The priest and the Levite took no notice of the wounded man. The Samaritan stopped, helped him, and made arrangements for his care.

Is the humanism the heart of the story? That is the first question that faces us. I believe the answer is a resounding "No!" The main point of the parable is not that we should be good to those in need, as important as that is. After all, many secular humanists who are unbelievers try to be good without any reference to God. They are not being elevated in this story. The heart of the story is the lawyer who believes in God, but does not want to put faith into action. Faith active in love, not humanism, is the heart of the story. That brings us to the three-question exchange in the first part of our story.

Three Questions That Set Up The Story

The lawyer in the story is an expert in the law of Moses and the Talmud. He is a believer. He comes to Jesus with a religious question, "What must I do to inherit eternal life?" (Luke 10:25). Jesus answers the lawyer's question with two questions, "What is written in the law? How do you read it?" (Luke 10:26). Notice that Jesus, a Jew, answers a question with a question.

Someone once asked a Jew, "Why do you Jews always answer a question with a question?" The Jew replied, "Why not?"

There is a good reason why Jesus answers the lawyer's question with a question. In Jewish tradition, the one who asks the question is in charge. The first question of the lawyer, while seemingly sincere, really means, "Let's talk about religion, maybe even debate a point or two of the law. What do you say?"

Jesus says, "No," to the invitation to discuss religion, just as he said, "No," to Nicodemus, a leader of the Jews, who had the same kind of religious discussion in mind when he approached him (John 3:1-15).

The lawyer answers the question about what is written in the law by quoting Deuteronomy 6:5 and Leviticus 19:18, "Love the Lord your God with all your heart and with all your soul and with all your strength and with all your mind," and "Love your neighbor as yourself." Jesus nails him with this statement: "Do this and you will live" (Luke 10:28).

The lawyer does not want to act on his faith in God by loving his neighbor. He just wants to talk about it. He is squirming as he tries to justify himself with a question. He is trying, vainly, to regain control of the situation. He asks a question, the Jewish way to gain control. "So who is my neighbor?" (Luke 10:29).

Jesus nails him with a story that never answers his question. Jesus never tells the lawyer who his neighbor is, except perhaps hinting that every needy person is a neighbor. Instead, he changes the verbalized question to the real question for the lawyer and all of us who claim to be Christians: "What does it mean to be a good neighbor?"

Jesus gives no definition to the word "neighbor." Definitions are for intellectual discussion. Definitions box in and limit meaning. The lawyer wants a definition to keep the theological discussion going. Jesus gives the lawyer a description that closes out the discussion and leads to the possibility of action.

In Hebrew thinking, description, not definition, is primary. Stories, not scientific analysis, carry the message. Parables are the chief teaching method of Jesus as he talks about the kingdom of God. Belonging to the kingdom of God by faith should always result in loving action. The kingdom of God means God's rule over our life for our own good. That is the one thing the lawyer in our story is trying to avoid: God's rule. Jesus goes for the jugular by telling a story with a hook in it.

The hook in the parable of the good Samaritan may catch us as it catches the lawyer. Many of us, like the lawyer, discuss religion instead of putting it into action. Many of us find it difficult to face the question of putting faith into action. One of the maladies of modern life is that many say that they believe in God, but do little or nothing about that belief. Often the connection between belief and behavior is not made. In other words, some people, like the lawyer, do not even intend to walk their talk. What difference does it make that we hear or read this parable? That is the hook that comes in the form of two questions at the end of the story. One of the questions is stated, one implied.

The Hook: Two Questions At The End

Jesus asks a question at the end of his story that has the power to reveal our malady of not putting faith into action. The point of the parable is not that we should be good humanitarians, but that we should believe in God in such a way that faith is active in love. The question I have been frequently asked, "Isn't an unchurched humanist just as good as a church-goer who is a hypocrite?" is the wrong question. The right question is, "After coming to faith in God through Jesus Christ, how can I do anything but show love for my neighbor?"

The question Jesus asks at the end of the story has a hook in it. It is intended to hook the lawyer. It is also intended to hook us. Jesus asks, "Which of these three (the priest, the Levite, or the Samaritan) do you think was a neighbor to the man who fell into the hands of robbers?" (Luke 10:36). The implied, unstated question in the conclusion of the story is, "What are you going to do about the faith that you claim you have?" These two questions can hook us for God.

Some years ago a lawyer named Chuck came into my office to discuss the possibility of joining the church. He had finished the pastor's class, an instruction class on the basics of the Christian faith, and said that he enjoyed it.

"I don't think that I will join the church," he said.

"That is your choice, of course, but can you tell me why?" I asked.

"I don't believe enough," he replied.

"The real question is not how much you believe, but what you are willing to do about what you believe," I suggested. *"More people act themselves into right ways of thinking than think themselves into right ways of acting."*

As it turned out, Chuck's wife was a Christian and a church member. Compared to her, he had just a little faith. He also had some doubts about the faith. "Chuck," I suggested, "it is not a matter of whether you have doubt or faith. We all have both doubt and faith. The real question is: 'Are you going to act on your doubt or your faith?' The question is not how much faith you have, but whether or not you are willing to act on whatever faith you have. Whatever gets your attention gets you. If you act on a little faith, it will grow. If you have a lot of faith, but don't act on it, it will fade. If you give your attention to your doubts and act on your doubts, they will get you."

"I never thought of it that way before," Chuck replied. Chuck joined the church. Within a year he was not only an active participant in our faith community, he was elected to the church council.

The hook in the end of the parable that can hook us for the Lord can be stated another way. After hearing or reading the story of the lawyer and the good Samaritan, the ultimate question is: "Christian, are you willing to 'go and do likewise'?" (Luke 10:37).

Points To Ponder

1. *The setting.* The narrow road from Jerusalem to Jericho was a notoriously dangerous road where robbers could strike quickly and escape quickly to the hills. Jesus' story was based on the experience that many people had of being robbed on this road.

2. *The characters.*
   a. *The scribe* who asked the question that gave rise to the story probably wore a little leather box on his wrist. That leather box was called a phylactery. It contained quotes from Scripture including Deuteronomy 6:4 and 11:3, telling the scribe to love the Lord his God, and Leviticus 19:18, bidding him to love his neighbor as himself. Jesus told him to look at his phylactery and follow what it says.

   b. *The traveler* was foolish for making this trip between Jerusalem and Jericho alone. He would have been wiser to travel with others. There is safety in numbers. Being alone, he was much more vulnerable to attack. After the attack, he was exposed to the elements and possible death.

   c. *The priest* was hurrying to get to the Temple to perform his religious duties. He may have thought that the man by the side of the road was dead in which case he would want to be sure not to touch him. Numbers 9:11 said that he who touched a dead man was unclean for seven days. If unclean, the priest could not do his ceremonial duty at the Temple. Temple ceremonies were more important to him than human need.

   d. *The Levite* had the tribe of Levi for a heritage. He was proud of that heritage. He may have thought that the man by the side of the road was a decoy, a trick often used by bandits. Self-absorbed in his lineage, he wanted to avoid risk at all costs. He missed a human need because of his pride.

32

e. *The Samaritan* was considered a villain in the minds of Jesus' Jewish hearers. Samaritans were a cross-breed race that emerged in the time of the Babylonian Captivity (587 B.C.) when the stronger Jews were deported to Babylon by Nebuchadnezzar, the conquering king of Babylon. The Jews who remained in Judah intermarried with pagans and compromised their heritage and monotheism. When Ezra, the spiritual leader of the returning Jews, called for purity of religion, the Jews looked down their noses in judgment at the Samaritans. In Jesus' time, a good Jew would walk miles out of his way to avoid the territory of Samaria which lay directly between Judah and Israel. The Samaritans were viewed as outsiders and heretics. That Jesus made a Samaritan the hero of this story was a shocking reversal for his hearers.

Questions For Personal Consideration
And/Or Group Discussion

1. What did you think when you first heard or read this parable as a youth?

2. What is your answer to the two questions at the end of Jesus' story?

3. What difference does this parable make in your personal life?

See **Digging Deeper**, p. 158, for further insights and application.

Chapter Three

Ready Or Not, Here I Come

Luke 12:13-21, 40

Years ago, as a child, I remember playing the game "Hide and Seek" on the streets of Chicago. One child would cover his or her eyes and count to ten while the others would go off and hide in the best hiding places they could find. At the count of ten, the first child would then say, "Ready or not, here I come."

That is the theme of Jesus' parable of the rich fool. Jesus is saying, "Ready or not, the day will come when your life will be demanded of you." Spiritual readiness helps us avoid the trap of covetousness and trivial pursuits and prepares us for eternity.

How can we avoid the trap of trivial pursuits and prepare for eternity? As you consider this story, ask yourself how to apply the truth of God to your own life.

Avoiding The Trap Of Trivial Pursuits Of Material Goods

I recently saw a bumper sticker on the back bumper of a big RV. It read, "At the end, the one with the most toys wins." Wins what? The gathering of expensive toys avails nothing. The pursuit of this world's toys is a trap. The Bible teaches that compared to eternal values, the material things of this world are trivial pursuits.

The Bible warns us about the danger of covetousness. The Bible also shows us how to avoid the dangers of seeking the things of this world as if they had lasting value.

First, pay more attention to God and his kingdom than to the things of this world. By comparison to God and his kingdom, the things of this world are trivial pursuits. That doesn't mean paying no attention to earning a good living, buying food and clothes, saving and investing, purchasing a car, or buying a home. It just means paying more attention to God than to all of these things. Saint Paul put it this way, "... We fix our eyes not on what is seen, but on what is unseen. For what is seen is temporary, but what is unseen is eternal" (2 Corinthians 4:18). How do we "fix our eyes on what is unseen," God's eternal values?

We fix our eyes on God through prayer. Prayer is not a way to get what you want from God. Rather, prayer is tuning into the station where God is speaking. Prayer means paying attention to God.

We fix our eyes on God by listening to and reading his Word. The Word is preached and taught at Christian churches every Sunday. Regular worship puts us in touch with God, his faith family, and his values.

We fix our eyes on God by renewing our minds. Saint Paul wrote, "Do not conform any longer to the pattern of this world, but be transformed by the renewal of your mind" (Romans 12:2). Seeing the difference between this world and the kingdom of God, renouncing the values of the one and setting the priority of the other is the way we open ourselves to the transforming power of God.

Right before the parable of the rich fool, Jesus says,

> *I tell you, my friends, do not be afraid of those who kill the body and after that can do no more. But I will show you whom you should fear: Fear him who, after the killing of the body, has power to throw you into hell. Yes, I tell you, fear him. Are not five sparrows sold for two pennies? Yet not one of them is forgotten by God. Indeed, the very hairs of your head are all numbered. Don't be afraid; you are worth more than many sparrows.*
>
> *I tell you, whoever acknowledges me before men, the Son of Man will also acknowledge him before the angels of God. But he who disowns me before men will be disowned before the angels of God.*
>
> — Luke 12:4-9

Greed causes us to forget that material goods last only for this life. Gathering the material goods of this world as our highest priority gets us into trouble. There are consequences to the priorities you set. Seek the kingdom of God before everything else. Jesus puts it this way:

> *Consider how the lilies grow. They do not labor or spin. Yet I tell you, not even Solomon in all his splendor was dressed like one of these. If that is how God clothes the grass of the field, which is here today, and tomorrow is thrown into the fire, how much more will he clothe you, O you of little faith! And do not set your heart on what you will eat or drink; do not worry about it. For the pagan world runs after all such things, and your Father knows that you need them. But seek his kingdom, and these things will be given to you as well.*
> — Luke 12:27-31

Second, as you become aware of the priority of God's kingdom, review your actions in the light of that priority. Apply the truths of the kingdom as the Bible reveals them.

Application is the hardest thing of all. For example, among other things, the practical application of kingdom truth has to do with money and possessions.

The presenting problem for Jesus telling the parable of the rich fool was a man asking Jesus to be the judge in a question of a family inheritance. It was customary among the Jews for the oldest son to inherit all the property at the death of the father. This protected small family farms from being divided into such small portions that eventually there would not be enough land for anyone to use for farming. The oldest son got everything. He was responsible for caring for the whole family. Apparently the man who approached Jesus was a younger brother who did not like the traditional arrangement. Jesus read the heart of the man. His problem was not that he was opposed to a Jewish tradition, but that greed had rooted itself in his heart.

It is very possible that the younger son believed in God and went to synagogue regularly. After all, he was there listening to the teachings of Jesus. The man's problem was not that he wasn't religious. It was that he did not apply biblical truth to practical problems because of an inner covetousness that he refused to overcome. That happens to many religious people. They know the truths of the Bible, but they do not apply these truths to their lives.

At a pastors' Bible study of this parable, all the pastors present agreed that at the time of death there are often divisions between family members about who gets what. "Death brings out the best and the worst in people," one older pastor said. "Usually the worst," another chimed in. "It even happens to Christians," said a third. "It happened to me when my parents died," said a fourth. "I am not proud of the way I acted. Something came over me. It was plain covetousness. I am ashamed of the way I acted toward my brothers and sisters. We squabbled. I should have been wiser and more spiritual. We have made up, but it took a long time."

Trivial pursuits based on greed often emerge at the time of a death in the family. Even when we know better, pursuit of property and money can bring out the worst in us, if we do not apply the truths we know to our lives in practical ways.

Apparently this is what was going on in the story of the man who asked for a judgment by Jesus. Jesus, seeing his greedy heart, exposed it by saying, "Man, who appointed me a judge or an arbiter between you and your brother? ... Watch out! Be on your guard against all kinds of greed; a man's life does not consist in the abundance of his possessions" (Luke 12:14-15). In telling the story of the rich fool Jesus exposed the tendency toward greediness in all of us. He also exposed the tendency to neglect the eternal values of God.

Embracing Eternal Values

The farmer in the story did not do anything wrong in executing his entrepreneurial plans. The crops were good. Farm goods were selling well. The money was rolling in. He tore down smaller storehouses and built bigger ones. So, what's the problem? The problem was in his attitude.

For eleven years, I was the senior pastor of a large church in Davenport, Iowa. Over fifty percent of the members were farmers or in the farm implement business. The first week I was in town, one of the farmers told me, "Pastor, this is rich bottom land of the Mississippi River. This is some of the best farmland in the world." With land like that, many of the hard-working farmers in and around Davenport prospered. What's the problem with prosperity? Nothing. Nothing is wrong with prosperity — not in the parable, nor among farmers in the Davenport area, not in our lives, *if* — and *if* is a big word — we have the right attitude about eternal values. What then is the "itch" for which Jesus supplies a "scratch" in the parable of the rich farmer?

The problem (the "itch") that is being addressed, here and in our lives, is the farmer's attitude, expressed in the farmer's thoughts, "You have plenty of good things laid up for many years. Take life easy; eat, drink, and be merry" (Luke 12:19). Prosperity can cause us to forget that God reads our minds. "Look at what I have accomplished. The bigger and better barns (houses or cars) will show my neighbors how much I have achieved. I will be the envy of the neighborhood." Oops! He (we) just stepped over the line. We can be prosperous as long as we remain grateful to God, humble toward other people, and remember that eternity is coming.

Jesus put it this way:

> *Do not store up for yourselves treasures on earth where moth and rust destroy, and where thieves break in and steal. But store up for yourselves treasures in heaven, where moth and rust do not destroy, and where thieves do not break in and steal. For where your treasure is, there will your heart be also.*   — Matthew 5:19

An old proverb says, "As a man thinks, so he acts." God knows what we are thinking. God knows the dangers of covetous thinking. That is why we have two commandments about covetousness. Jesus drove this point home in his parable of the fool who was rich in material things, but not rich in the things of God. The rich fool in the parable never saw beyond himself and never saw beyond this life.

Many years ago a note was found near some skeletons near a dried-up well in Arizona. The note was written by some gold prospectors. It said:

We are out of water.
This well is dry.
We are out of food.
The Indians have us surrounded.
But we've got the gold!

How much good did the gold do them when they died? They never saw beyond themselves and never saw beyond this world.

A man and his new Cadillac convertible were being lowered into a grave according to his wishes. One of the gravediggers was heard to comment: "What a way to go!" Really? What difference will an expensive automobile make when we have to face God? In eternity the questions will not be: "How much money did you make? How big was your house? How expensive was your car?" The question will be: "How much did you love me?" The rich fool who was buried in his Cadillac convertible never saw beyond himself and never saw beyond this life.

A pastor tells how, during World War II, he was standing at a big gaping hole in the ground in Hamburg, Germany, thinking about the foolishness and pain of war. He looked into the hole where once several buildings had stood. He was thinking about people who had died in the war. Suddenly he became aware that a woman was standing beside him crying. She was one of his parishioners. "That was our home," she said. "My husband died there."

"I'm so sorry," the pastor said. "I wish that I could have helped your husband more."

"You helped more than you will ever know," she said. "You helped prepare my husband for eternity." That pastor helped his parishioner see beyond himself and beyond this life.

Isn't preparing people for eternity what life is all about?

The rich fool did not get it. We are invited to listen carefully to the Word of God in this parable so that we do get it. We will all die. That is the point of Jesus' words in Luke 12:20.

Death plays the child's game. "1-2-3-4-5-6-7-8-9-10. Ready or not, here I come."

You fool.
Tonight, you fool.
Ready or not,
Here I come.
Tonight. Tonight. Tonight.

Points To Ponder

1. *Disputes about money?* In Palestine, it was not uncommon for people to take disputes to their rabbis. Jesus refused to get involved in the dispute between brothers. Instead, he used the request of one of the brothers as a point of departure for a challenging story about wrong priorities about materialism.

2. *Riches?* Most of us do not think of ourselves as wealthy, but by the world's standards, most Americans are rich. The potential problem lies in how we view what we have, not how much we have.

3. *Stewardship?* Stewardship of possessions can be defined as what we do with our lives after we say, "Yes," to Jesus Christ as Lord and Savior. The stewardship of money means that we don't just see ourselves and this world, but that we see beyond this world to the eternal values of God and give of our time, talents, and treasures for the work of God and to meet the needs of others.

Questions For Personal Consideration
And/Or Group Discussion

1. Did you ever play "Hide and Seek" as a child? What memories do you have?

2. How can making a good living or seeking riches be trivial pursuits?

3. What was the rich fool's problem?

4. What is the warning of Jesus in this parable?

See **Digging Deeper**, p. 159, for further insights and application.

Chapter Four

Four Warnings

Luke 13:18-30

Have you ever seen WARNING! signs on a highway? They are trying to tell you that something up ahead is potentially dangerous. What is up ahead? Dangerous curves. Quick stops. Steep hills. Traffic lights. In Luke 13:18-30 Jesus is giving us four warning signs about the kingdom of God. If we do not heed the warnings, we may miss the coming of the kingdom in our lives. The kingdom of God is so important that it was the driving force in our lives since it was the highest priority in Jesus' life.

Theologian Carl Braaten describes the highest priority in Jesus' life like this:

> The "kingdom of God" was the central theme in the entire message of Jesus. All three synoptic Gospels picture Jesus as an itinerant preacher from Galilee announcing the good news of the kingdom of God (Mark 1:15; Matthew 4:23; Luke 4:43) ... The kingdom of God was more than a concept in the mind of Jesus set forth in speech. It was the driving force of his whole career.[1]

In his book, *Sign of the Kingdom*, theologian Leslie Newbiggen urges us to look for the signs that warn us about various aspects of the kingdom of God. "The kingdom of God was the central theme of Jesus ... The foretaste of the kingdom of God, the *arroban*, is the gift of the Holy Spirit."[2] *Arroban* is a Greek term used in the New Testament to describe a foretaste, a preview, or an advance notice

43

of something important up ahead. Are we heeding the warning signs that Jesus gives so that we do not miss the kingdom?

Jesus' words in Luke 13:18-30 are warning signs about the kingdom of God. Jesus gives four down-to-earth illustrations of what the kingdom of God is like so that we will not miss what is up ahead. He says that the kingdom of God is like: 1) a mustard seed (Luke 13:18); 2) a bit of yeast in a loaf of bread (13:20); 3) a narrow door (13:24); and 4) a great banquet with people coming from all directions to attend (13:29).

The Kingdom Is Like A Mustard Seed

In chapter 1 of this book, we considered the parable of the mustard seed as it is found in Matthew 13:31-33. There we spoke of it as a snapshot reminder. Here we look at these words as a warning sign. *Warning! Since the kingdom starts small, you are in danger of overlooking it!*

God's kingdom may be missed since, like a mustard seed, it starts out small. Although it looks insignificant, don't be fooled. A mustard seed can grow to ten to twelve feet in height. The kingdom of God may initially seem small and inconsequential from an earthly point of view, but it can grow to become the greatest driving force in the hearts of God's children.

Baptism initiates us into the kingdom of God. It is like planting a small seed. That seed can grow to great stature if it is nurtured. Many overlook baptism to their own peril.

A grandmother named Mary wanted to help her grandson Adam remember his baptism and thus remember his identity as a child of God. From the time the child was born and baptized, each time the grandmother saw him, she made the sign of the cross on his forehead and said the baptismal words, "In the name of the Father and of the Son and of the Holy Spirit." At age six, Adam drew a picture of himself to send to his grandmother. The picture included a cross on his forehead.

At age 25 Adam was ordained as a pastor. As he made the sign of the cross at the end of the ordination service, he remembered how his grandmother had made that sign on his forehead when he was a child.

At age 45 Adam became a bishop in the church. He made the sign of the cross and said the words, "In the name of the Father, and of the Son, and of the Holy Spirit," at the end of the consecration service. In his heart he thanked God for his grandmother who had continually reminded him that he was a child of God.

Small beginnings can grow into mature spirituality if we heed the warning that since the kingdom starts small and seems insignificant, we must be careful so that we do not overlook it.

The Kingdom Of God Is Like A Small Bit Of Yeast

This parable was also considered in chapter one of this book. There we spoke of it as a snapshot of what the kingdom of God is like. Here we speak of it as a warning sign. *Warning! Since the kingdom works quietly and slowly, be careful not to neglect it just because you do not see it working.*

Leaven causes bread to rise. When added to ordinary lives, the leaven of the kingdom of God causes ordinary people to rise above their circumstances and become extraordinary witnesses. God makes the change through the power of his Holy Spirit.

Marion was raised in a Christian home. She went to Sunday school and church regularly as a child. As a teenager she was confirmed and participated in the youth group at church. She taught Sunday school for a while. The leaven of the kingdom of God was quietly working in Marion's heart.

Marion married a Christian man. Together they grew in love for God, church, and one another. When a child was born of the union, tragedy struck. The baby was deaf. That would be enough to turn some people away from the Lord. Not Marion. She started to help deaf children learn about God in a special education class she started at her church.

Then tragedy struck again. Marion discovered that she had cancer. She told me, "For three months I could not eat. The cancer — three tumors in the small intestine area — was hidden so deep that the doctors could not find it. At the same time, I temporarily lost my hearing. It was a hard time, but a time for which I am grateful. John, my husband, was there. So was Jesus. I survived. Since then I have been working with cancer patients, trying to help them accept their condition and accept Jesus as Lord. The cancer gave me an opportunity to serve others."

It all started small like a little leaven in bread dough. Marion rose above her circumstances. She became an extraordinary witness for Christ.

The Kingdom Of God Is Like A Narrow Door

Warning! Since the door is narrow, make every effort to enter it while it is open. This is a parallel passage to Matthew 7:13-14 where Jesus says that the gate is small and the road is narrow that leads to life while the gate is wide and the road is broad that leads to destruction. Both passages deal with the cost of discipleship.

In answer to the question, "Are only a few people going to be saved?" (Luke 13:22-23), Jesus pictures a narrow door. While narrow, this door is open to all who will accept the invitation to come in. Don't stand there and debate how many people will get in. Come in yourself. Become a disciple (follower) of Jesus. Invite others to come in and become disciples.

Dietrich Bonhoeffer was a Lutheran pastor and theologian. He was martyred under Adolf Hitler at end of World War II. His discipleship cost him his life. He refused to acknowledge Hitler as *Der Fuhrer* (the Lord) because he confessed Christ as Lord. It is easy to say, "I believe in God." That costs nothing. It is easy to join a church. That costs little. To live as a disciple under the lordship of Christ means submission to the rule of God. Cheap grace, Bonhoeffer says, is grace without commitment. Costly grace means commitment to Jesus as Lord. Be careful. There are many wide doors opened to you in life. Dangers lurk there. We are invited to enter the narrow door to the kingdom of God while it is open and commit ourselves to Jesus, his works and his ways.

Small seeds like mustard seeds begin the work of God in us. Quiet but steady work, like leaven in a loaf of bread, produces great results. Entering a small and narrow door when invited leads to discipleship under the lordship of Jesus Christ. When you enter the narrow door, you will be surprised to discover that the kingdom of God is a party.

The Kingdom Of God Is Like A Great Party

Warning! Since most people think about Christianity in terms of doom and gloom and obedience to rules and regulations, they miss the invitation to the surprise party. Jesus says, "People will come from east and west and north and south, and will take their places at the feast in the kingdom of God" (Luke 13:29). The surprise is that "there are those who are last who will be first, and first who will be last" (Luke 13:30).

In his book, *The Kingdom of God Is a Party*, Tony Campolo describes the banquet of God like this:

> *Everybody was invited to the party, from widows who hadn't had a fun night out for a year, to poor kids who couldn't have come up with ticket money to whatever was the ancient equivalent of Disneyland. Prostitutes and tax collectors were invited. So what if their reputations were questionable? When it is a really good party, you forget all that stuff.*[3]

The kingdom of God is a really good party, hosted by God, for anyone, of all colors and kinds, who will humbly accept the invitation. The Pharisees and Sadducees were so puffed up with what they thought was their own goodness and righteousness that they could not get through the narrow door into the party. That is why these leaders, who thought of themselves as first in the religion parade, wound up last.

Pay attention to the warning signs. Accept the invitation to the great banquet and come. You will have a wonderful time.

Points To Ponder

1. *Front-end context.* Jesus humiliated his opponents who were criticizing him for the Sabbath healing of a woman crippled for eighteen years (Luke 13:10-17). This conflict set up the four warnings of Luke 13:18-30.

2. *Back-end context.* In Luke 13:30 Jesus says that there will be a reversal of the first and the last. The Pharisees and Sadducees, who are first in the religion parade of their day, will be last. Little people who pay attention to the Lord's words and believe him, like the crippled woman of Luke 13:10-17, will be first.

3. *The tree as a place of shelter.* In the east, one of the symbols of a great empire was a mighty tree. Subject nations found shelter in its branches. See Ezekiel 31:6; 17:13. All kinds of people and nations, including the Gentiles, will come together in the kingdom of God according to Luke 13:29.

4. *The kingdom of God has small beginnings.* Jesus teaches that small beginnings do not prohibit great growth (Luke 13:18-19). He also teaches that the kingdom of God works from something being added to the dough that then works from the inside out (Luke 13:20-21).

5. *Luke 13:22-30.* In the strictest sense, these verses are not parables, but similes.

48

Questions For Personal Consideration
And/Or Group Discussion

1. Have you ever gotten into trouble when you ignored a warning sign on a road?

2. How have you seen the kingdom of God starting small and then becoming large?

3. How have you seen the kingdom of God working slowly but surely in your life or the life of someone you know?

4. How do you see the kingdom of God as a great celebration?

See **Digging Deeper**, p. 160, for further insights and application.

Chapter Five

Party Humility And Hospitality

Luke 14:1, 7-14

Some years ago I saw a picture in the *Chicago Tribune* which really made me stop and think about the values of this world as contrasted with the values of the kingdom of God as described in the Bible. The picture was of a fire that had taken place at the Glenview Naval Air Station. Damage was estimated at $10,000,000. The picture was of an iron staircase leading up. The staircase had survived the fire. That's all that was left. Everything else around it was burned. The second floor was gone. The title of the picture was "Stairway to Nowhere."

In his parable in Luke 14:1, 7-14 Jesus offers an alternative staircase, "The Staircase to Heaven." He is saying, "Come to the party called the kingdom of God with humility and when you throw a party, do it with genuine hospitality." Graced in the social mores of the time, Jesus reaches far beyond etiquette to tell us about the heart of the kingdom of God. While these words are aimed directly at the Pharisees who were holding a party that Jesus attended, they reach across time to touch our lives today.

Humility

Self-seeking is a stairway to nowhere. Genuine humility is a stairway to heaven. Jesus says, "When someone invites you to a wedding feast, do not take the place of honor ... Everyone who exalts himself will be humbled and he who humbles himself will be exalted" (Luke 14:8, 11).

Guests arriving early might choose places of honor and then be told to go to a lower place. But more than seats of honor at a

51

wedding banquet is at stake in this story. This story is a warning about what keeps people out of the banquet called the kingdom of God.

Exalting yourself keeps you out of the kingdom of God. Scheming for places of honor reveals a fatal flaw in character. Elbowing your way past others shows that there is inordinate, sinful ambition in the heart. Self-seeking, the malady of the Pharisees in our story, is also the malady of many people today.

Self-seeking in the "Me Generation" is often presented as the only way to go. The secular creeds of the "Me Generation" are:
"If you don't push yourself forward, nobody will."
"Those who do not step forward should step aside."
"Move over; here comes Number One!"
"If you don't take care of Number One, who will?"

Jesus provides the biblical corrective for self-seeking when he says, "When you are invited to a wedding feast, do not take the place of honor." The wedding feast he is talking about is the kingdom of God. Self-seeking will keep you out. Self-seeking is a stairway to nowhere. Humility is the attitude that is appropriate for those who are on their way to the Great Banquet of God. Humility is the proper etiquette for the feast called the kingdom of God.

Societal etiquette means good manners and appropriate behavior from the point of view of good traditions. Societal etiquette means doing the right and proper thing according to convention and custom. Societal etiquette means honoring the mores and manners of a society or group. This parable is not about societal etiquette.

This parable is about the kingdom of God etiquette called humility. Humility does not mean crunching down lower than you really are. It means stretching out to your fullest, but doing it before God so that you see just how small you really are. Humility is like standing at the bottom of the Grand Canyon and looking up.

Saint Paul speaks of humility as a sign of the saved in Philippians 2:5-11.

> *Your attitude should be the same as that of Christ Jesus:*
> *Who, being in very nature God, did not consider equal-*
> *ity with God something to be grasped, but made himself*

nothing, taking the very nature of a servant, being made in human likeness. And being found in appearance as a man, he humbled himself and became obedient to death —even death on a cross! Therefore God exalted him to the highest place and gave him the name that is above every name, that at the name of Jesus every knee should bow, in heaven and on earth and under the earth, and every tongue confess that Jesus Christ is Lord, to the glory of God the Father.

In the Middle Ages, a monk decided to preach on humility. His sermon was eloquent in spite of the fact that he used very few words. It was an evening service. When it came time for the sermon, the monk took a candle and walked beneath the huge crucifix in the sanctuary. Then he moved the candle from wound to wound on the hands, the feet, and the side of Jesus, pausing before each wound for a few moments. When he was done, he simply said, "Behold what has been done for you."

Jesus speaks of the foolishness of the party-goers who try to assert themselves and take places of honor. He shows us the way of humility as an alternate to futility.

Hospitality
Always wanting to be paid back, the world's way of hospitality, is a staircase to nowhere. Genuine hospitality is a stairway to heaven.

In our story Jesus says, "When you give a luncheon or dinner, do not invite your friends, your brothers or relatives or your rich neighbors; if you do, they may invite you back and so you will be repaid. But when you give a banquet, invite the poor, the crippled, the lame, the blind and you will be blessed" (Luke 14:12-14).

This portion of the parable deals with the kingdom etiquette of hospitality. The etiquette Jesus speaks about is not a new set of rules from Emily Post or Amy Vanderbilt. Jesus' words about hospitality are substantial, fundamental, and foundational for believers. Inviting people who cannot pay you back to a party is a sign that you understand the nature of faith. Selfless service to strangers is the theme of many biblical verses and stories.

53

The *New International Version* translation of Hebrews 13:2 says, "Do not forget to entertain strangers, for by so doing some people have entertained angels without knowing it." Another translation says, "Do not neglect hospitality to strangers...." In the original Greek, the word we translate "hospitality" is *philoxenia*. *Philoxenia* means treating strangers as if they are angels from God.

In Genesis 18:1-15, Abraham shows that type of hospitality to three strangers who come to his tent in the desert. He offers food, drink, and shelter to the three men. In the midst of eating, the three ask about Sarah, Abraham's wife. One of the three then predicts that Sarah, who was barren, will have a son within a year. When Sarah hears this prediction, she laughs. Nine months later she bears a son. Abraham and Sarah name him Isaac, which means laughter. The stranger who predicted the birth was an angel of God. When we show genuine hospitality, not looking for anything in return, God has a way of showing up with blessings and joy.

Of course, you cannot show hospitality in order to get those blessings. The attitude of seeking to get something back for your hospitality is a stairway to nowhere. That is the point of the Abraham story and the parable of Jesus. It is only selfless service to the stranger that produces joy and laughter. To seek rewards for being hospitable is to miss the point and miss the rewards.

God calls us to do good for people because so much good has been done to us. Selfless acts of hospitality are signs of the saved. In another kingdom parable, Jesus puts it this way, "As you have done it for the least of these, you have done it to me."

Jesus' message is inspirational. The poor, the crippled, the lame, and the blind in Luke 14:13 are important because they cannot pay you back for what you do for them. Legalists keep track and want to be paid back. People filled with pride keep track of the score. Christians are called to be generous and gracious hosts and hostesses like God. Max Lucado puts it this way: "The sign of the saved is their love of the least."[4]

Jesus' message is the opposite of the world's message. Jesus' message is disturbing to those who live by the world's standards. Some years ago I shared this value system of humility and hospitality with no eye toward reward with a business man. His reaction was, "If that is what Christianity is all about, I want no part of it. I am a self-made man. When I do something for someone, I expect to be paid back in kind." Being a self-made man with a view toward pay back may work in business, but it does not work in life. Jesus' disciples are expected to be like him, showing humility and hospitality.

Jesus' message is revolutionary. It upsets the way we normally think. "What is the last book in the Bible?" a Sunday school teacher asked her fifth grade class. One of the ten-year-old boys quickly replied, "The book of Revolution."

"Johnny, that's Revelation, not Revolution," said the teacher. Just then the bell rang and the class left.

The following Sunday the teacher said, "I've been thinking all week about Johnny's answer. The last book of the Bible is a kind of revolutionary book. It speaks of the spiritual revolution in people who follow the revolutionary values of Jesus. Jesus turns the world's selfish values upside down."

"Does anyone know who wrote this revolutionary book?"

Johnny's hand was up. "Was it Saint Paul Revere?"

Johnny was wrong about Saint Paul Revere, but in a certain sense he was right about Christianity being revolutionary. Genuine humility and genuine hospitality turn the values of the world upside down.

The world's way is a stairway to nowhere.

Points To Ponder

1. *Front-side context.* Luke 14:1-6 sets up the parable about proud guests and inhospitable hosts. As Jesus heals a man with dropsy on the Sabbath day, he is under the scrutiny of the Pharisees and Scribes. What they do not know is that they are under the scrutiny of God for their staggering lack of a sense of proportion of what is important and what is not. Petty rules and regulations are nothing compared to human need. These religious leaders have their priorities all mixed up.

55

2. *Back-side context.* Luke 14:15-23 contains the parable of the Great Banquet. In the parable of humility and hospitality, Jesus is saying, "Compare your attitudes to the Great Banquet of God. You won't like the comparison, but if you listen to what I am saying, you will learn what God expects. What God expects is what God does. Pharisees and Scribes, you are missing the point altogether."

3. *Luke 14:12-14 examines motives.* There are many reasons to throw a party. Self-interest, to feel superior, or to do one's duty are not acceptable motives for hosting a party or living a life in the sight of God. The motive that Jesus models and promotes is joyous generosity to those who cannot repay. If you do something good with an eye on what others will do for you, you have missed the point.

Questions For Personal Consideration And/Or Group Discussion

1. What comes to your mind when you picture a stairway to nowhere?

2. Name some people you either know or know about who demonstrate Christ-like humility.

3. Name some people you either know or know about who show genuine hospitality.

See **Digging Deeper**, p. 161, for further insights and application.

Chapter Six

RSVP: Avoiding
Attractive Distractions

Luke 14:15-24

In this story Jesus warns his hearers not to miss the opportunity to join the festivities of faith no matter what else is happening. Specifically, he aims the warning at Jewish leaders who are missing the party because of stubborn resistance. He predicts that people of all colors and kinds will come in because they accept the invitation. Gentiles will come in and fill up the places at the party left by those who were originally invited but did not come because they had seemingly good excuses.

Jesus said, "Come, for everything is now ready" (Luke 14:17). But they all alike began to make excuses. The attractive distractions of this world can keep you out of God's party called the kingdom of God.

In this parable, the attractive distractions that keep people away from the festival of faith are the distraction of business, the distraction of new things, and the distraction of good things.

The Distraction Of Business

There is the excuse of the demanding claims of business. "I have bought a field, and I must go and see it. Please excuse me" (Luke 14:18). The first man was caught in the attractive distraction of business. Many people are.

Buying and selling land or houses or any property is demanding work. A friend recently said, "I'm getting out of the real estate business. It takes all my time. I don't have time for church, family,

57

or friends." Another friend who sells automobiles told me that the demands of a car salesman are very stressful. "You work a ten-hour shift and sometimes no customers show up all day. Then in the last ten minutes, three show up all at once and none of them buys." Someone who recently refinanced a home said, "The paper work is mind-blowing. I'm worn out." A small business owner said, "We are always on the brink of disaster."

In other words, we can sympathize with the man in our story who got all caught up in the claims of business. Even in simpler times, buying a piece of land put high demands on people. Then and now, business demands can lay claims on us and distract us from coming to the banquet called the kingdom of God. Business demands are viewed here as an unacceptable reason to miss the banquet feast.

William Barclay, the New Testament scholar, writes about the insult involved in the making of excuses for not coming to a banquet in the first century.

> *In Palestine, when a man made a feast, the day was announced long beforehand and the invitations were sent out and accepted; but the hour was not announced; and when the day came and all things were ready, servants were sent out to summon the already invited guests. To accept the invitation beforehand and then to refuse it when the day came was a grave insult.*[5]

There is a warning in our story. There is judgment. There is also sadness on the part of the host. The opulence of the kingdom banquet magnifies the enormity of the rejection. The most wonderful banquet in the world is missed by some because of the distraction of business. Others miss the banquet because of the distraction of new things.

The Distraction Of New Things

The second man offers this excuse for not attending: "I have just bought five yoke of oxen and I'm on my way to try them out. Please excuse me" (Luke 14:19).

It is not likely that any of us have recently purchased oxen, but the novelty of new things is familiar territory to all of us. The distraction of a new car, a new house, a new cabin, a new boat or RV, a new TV or VCR, a new vacation trip, or a new friend can capture our time and attention and keep us out of the kingdom of God because these things seem more important at the time. "Whatever gets your attention, gets you," E. Stanley Jones observed. New things easily get our attention, unless we focus on God and keep possessions in proper perspective.

I live in California. Recreation dominates the thinking of many people here. Many say, "I used to go to church, but now I go off to the mountains, the lakes, or the many interesting places in our area. I am too busy for church."

A friend recently gave me this anonymous article:

"No Excuse Sunday"

In order to make it possible for everyone to attend church next Sunday, we are planning a special "No Excuse Sunday."

1. *Cots will be placed in the vestibule for those who say, "Sunday is my only day for sleeping in."*

2. *Eye drops will be available for those whose eyes are tired from watching too much TV too late on Saturday night.*

3. *We will have steel helmets for those who believe the roof will cave in if they show up for church.*

4. *Blankets will be furnished for those who complain that the church is too cold. Fans will be on hand for those who say the church is too hot.*

5. *We will have hearing aids for people who say, "The pastor does not talk loud enough." There will be cotton for those who say, "The pastor talks too loud."*

59

6. *Scorecards will be available for those who wish to count the hypocrites.*

7. *We guarantee that some relatives will be present for those who like to have company on Sunday.*

8. *There will be TV dinners available for those who claim they can't go to church and cook too.*

9. *One section of the church will have some trees and grass for those who see God in nature or on the golf course.*

10. *The sanctuary will be decorated with both Christmas poinsettias and Easter lilies to create a familiar environment for those who have never seen the church without them.*

Excuses about church are not the same as excuses about the kingdom of God because the kingdom and the church are not the same. The kingdom comes to people through the preaching of the gospel in the church, but the church is not the kingdom. At best, the church gives us a preview or foretaste of the kingdom. While the church and the kingdom are not identical, excuses for not coming to the one run parallel to excuses for not entering the other. In this parable Jesus warns us about the danger of making excuses when God sends out the invitation to come.

There is judgment in Jesus' story of the wedding feast. There is also sadness. Jesus wants us to have joy. He wants us to partake in the festivities of the kingdom. He is saddened when the novelty of the new distracts us. He is also saddened when people pass up an opportunity for the best when they are distracted by good things.

The Distraction Of The Good

It is possible to see that the excuse of business priorities of the first man and the excuse of materialistic priorities of the second man are condemned in Jesus' story. We are shocked to hear that Jesus is just as hard on the third man who offers the excuse that he

60

has just gotten married. "I just got married, so I can't come," said the third man in the parable. Isn't that a good excuse? Aren't marriage and family high priorities in the Bible?

The Bible says, "When a man is newly married, he shall not go out with the army or be charged with any business; he shall be free at home one year, to be happy with his wife whom he has taken" (Deuteronomy 24:5, RSV). The Bible teaches the priority of marriage and family over many things, but the Bible never asserts the priority of marriage and family over God.

Jesus knew the Bible's high priority of the newly married to explore the wonders of intimacy, relationship, and sex. Jesus believed in family values, but he also knew that anything, even good things like family values, can become idols.

As business and material goods can become idols, so can a spouse. An idol is anything, other than God, that you put in first place in your life. What is in first place in your life? If the answer is your wife or husband, you are in trouble. The only thing that works as the highest priority is God. That is why the third excuse is no better than the first two. To love a spouse or children below God makes the family second only to what is absolutely primary: God's kingdom. Jesus' story brings us face to face with the only thing that is ultimate in life: God's banquet is the celebration of his rule over us for our own good. Only there do we find ultimate fulfillment. That is why there is singing and dancing, and fellowship and joy at the banquet called the kingdom of God.

A spouse dies. Children leave home. Only God stays with us throughout life. If we put an ultimate priority on family, we will always be disappointed. Family is in second place, below God.

When you receive an invitation to come to this party called the kingdom of God, no excuse will do. Come to this party and find ultimate fulfillment in this life and eternal life in the next.

The invitation reads, "RSVP." What is your response?

Points To Ponder

1. *Luke 14:15.* When Jesus' hearer at a party asks about happiness in the kingdom feast, he is referring to the Messianic banquet when the golden days of the new age arrive. The Jews believed that at this time God would dramatically break into history and elevate the Jews. Like most Jews of his time, this man was thinking that the kingdom feast was for Jews only. In this parable, Jesus shocks his hearers by saying that the Jews are not the only guests at his banquet. Many of the originally invited guests rejected the invitation to come to the kingdom feast.

2. *Luke 14:23.* "Make them come in" or as another translation puts it, "Compel them to come in," at times has been misunderstood by Christians to mean forcing people into the church. This verse was used in defense of the Spanish Inquisition. Instead, the verse means having a passion and priority for witnessing to the faith with love. Compulsion to witness comes out of love. See 2 Corinthians 5:14.

3. *The kingdom of God as a banquet.* This symbol shows that the kingdom as Jesus pictures it is the happiest, most joyful thing we can imagine. This emphasis is a wonderful corrective to the notion that the Christian faith is a matter of duty, doom, and gloom. Tony Campolo's *The Kingdom of God Is a Party* is a helpful book to help restore the nature of the Christian faith as a joyful experience.

Questions For Personal Consideration
And/Or Group Discussion

1. Do you like parties or not?

2. How is the kingdom of God party different from other parties?

3. What kinds of excuses have you heard people make for not participating in the faith family?

See **Digging Deeper**, p. 162, for further insights and application.

Chapter Seven

The Wonderful Party
And The Strange Guests

Luke 14:15-24

In chapter six we looked at this parable from the point of view of the excuses that people make for not coming to God's banquet. The apparently legitimate excuses were plausible lies. Here, looking at the same parable, we have a different focus. Our focus here is the nature of the party and the attitude of the strange guests who come. The apparently wonderful party is better than we can imagine. The apparently strange guests have one thing in common that makes it possible to accept the king's invitation.

The Wonderful Banquet

What is heaven like? In the Bible, the most frequent description of heaven is not golden streets and silver lamps. The most frequent description is not angels playing harps forever. The most frequent description of heaven is that it is like a great banquet. That banquet is called the kingdom of God.

You may be an extrovert who loves parties or an introvert who dislikes them. Whatever your personality, you will love the party called the kingdom of God. At this party the forever family of God meets and eats, with no calories. Of course, the point of a great banquet is not really food. It is the fellowship and relationship of the family members with the Father and with one another that counts.

Thanksgiving or Christmas family dinners are generally wonderful, memorable times for families. People come from great distances to be at these festivities. Family ties are strengthened. Old friendships are renewed. New ones are made. The grandchildren get to know one another. Of course, some family get-togethers are spoiled by too much drinking, too much fighting, or too many old wounds opened, but even when these things happen, we know that festival family banquets are supposed to be better than this.

The kingdom of God banquet is better than any family gathering or party we have ever attended. People really get to know the Father better. They discover his loving heart and the meaning of the experiences they have had. They overcome obstacles and repair old wounds. They forgive and are forgiven. They are refreshed and filled with love. They give love to those who don't deserve it and receive love from those who from a human point of view should not give it.

The kingdom of God banquet is our destiny. We were created for moments such as this. When we experience forgiveness and love in this life, it is a preview of coming attractions. It is a foretaste of things to come. Who could ask for anything more?

The point of this parable is that this is God's party. No doubt about it, it is better than we deserve. It is far beyond what we can imagine. "No eye has seen; no ear has heard, no mind conceived what God has prepared for those who love him" (1 Corinthians 2:9).

That is why the lame excuses we discussed in the last chapter are so insulting. This host will not accept any excuses because he knows what we too easily forget. The best is yet to come. The best has been in preparation for a long time. The best is ready. Only the best will do. The Father has prepared this banquet for you. No matter who you are or what you have done, if you hear the invitation and come, you are welcomed.

The Strange Guests

"Go out quickly into the streets and alleys of the town and bring in the poor, the crippled, the blind and the lame" (Luke 14:21b). Strange guests for such a grand party! The point is that anyone can come. Anyone! That point is made a second time when the host is told that his order to invite the nobodies has been fulfilled and that there is still room. "Then the master told his servant,

66

'Go out to the roads and country lanes and make them come in, so that my house will be full' " (Luke 14:23). Another translation says, "Compel them to come in." In other words, go out with passion to find everyone and be sure that everyone knows that he or she is invited to the Great Banquet of God.

Who is out there on the country lanes and sleeping in the bushes near the roads? The bums and drunks, the tramps and transients live in such places. They are all invited to come to the party. As long as you hear the invitation, believe the host's words and come, you are welcomed.

While all of this is true, to understand this text, we must also understand the context of this passage. The front-side context of Luke 14:15-24 includes Luke 13:22 and forward where Jesus says that we must strive to enter the narrow gate. Many go the broad way to destruction. Few find the narrow gate and go through it. Doesn't this passage contradict the parable about the open, inclusive invitation?

The front-side context also includes Luke 13:34 and forward where Jesus weeps over Jerusalem because the people there did not know the day of visitation. He laments because as a hen will cover her chicks with her wings to protect them, so God will cover his own. Yet, "You would not come," Jesus says. The contrast between this lamenting on the one hand and the open, inclusive invitation of the parable on the other, is disturbing, isn't it? What is going on in the lamentation over Jerusalem?

In North Dakota it is said that in a prairie fire a mother hen will cover her chicks to keep them from burning. Following a fire, North Dakota farmers often find the charred remains of mother hens. The protected chicks are still alive because of the sacrifice of the mother hens. That is how much God cares.

The front-side context of the narrow gate and the lamentation over Jerusalem are not a contradiction of the parable of the open door and the inclusive invitation. The front side context and the text are a paradox, two truths held in tension by the Bible. The door to the kingdom is open. The invitation to come is inclusive. The trouble is that many ignore the invitation and break the heart of God by doing so.

Anyone can come to the banquet, even the bums, if they appreciate the sacrifice that is involved in extending the invitation to them. Anyone can enter the narrow gate to the kingdom. But you cannot enter the narrow gate if you take God for granted. If you strive to understand what has been done for you, even if you do not fully understand it, you will be welcomed, but assuming that you have a right to salvation keeps you out.

The back-side context of Luke 14:15-24 says the same thing. In Luke 14:25-34, we hear about the cost of discipleship. This initially seems to contradict the open invitation of the parable of the great banquet. "If anyone comes to me and does not hate his father and mother, his wife and children, his brothers and sisters — yes, even his own life — he cannot be my disciple," Jesus says (Luke 14:26). To understand these words, we must understand that in the original Greek text, "hate" means "loving far less." In other words, the person who comes to the banquet of the kingdom must see that the invitation of the host has such a high priority that every other loyalty pales by comparison.

A builder counting the cost of building a tower or a king counting the cost of going to war, used in Luke 14:25-34, are illustrations of submitting to the authority of the host who invites us to his party. At first, submitting to this host seems like too high a requirement to come to this party. On further examination, this emphasis on submission can be seen as the fulfillment of our destiny to come under the lordship of our Creator. Submission is the hardest thing of all and the one thing necessary. We were created to come under the Lord. This is what the kingdom of God is all about. God's rule over us is for our own good. God is not some eastern potentate who is mad with power and insists that everyone bow down to him to fulfill his ego needs. God is our Father who knows what we too easily forget: that if we are not under his lordship, we will be under the lordship of someone or something else. We have no choice of whether or not we will be ruled, only who will be the ruler. Only the one who invites us to the kingdom of God party will rule us for our own good. Every other ruler is an idol.

The bums in the bushes have tried other gods that do not work. They have crashed as they have tried and failed at running their own lives. They have failed as they made other gods, followed them, and discovered misery and trouble at the hands of idols. The bums in the bushes and the other strange guests are more likely to respond to the kingdom invitation than the socially elite. The bums know that they have failed by the world's standards. Martin Luther once put it this way: "It is God's nature to create out of nothing. If you are not yet nothing, God won't make anything out of you."

Is it only the bums who can get in? Of course not! Anyone can come, even the most successful persons in the world, but they must remember that in terms of salvation they too are lost. Only those who know that they are lost listen. No one is worthy of the invitation. The invitation to the kingdom of God party comes by the grace of the king.

The problem with most of us is that we compare ourselves to other people and conclude that we are better than many, much better than some. This parable is intended to call us to compare ourselves to God. When you compare yourself to God, you are a bum. When you discover that status, you realize just how precious the invitation to come to God's party is. You have not earned the invitation. You do not deserve the invitation. The invitation comes by the grace of the king.

This is the king's party. You are just one of many flawed and sinful guests who have only one thing in common. You got here by grace, not personal virtue, good works, or status in society. You are one of the lost. Only the lost listen.

Come to the party called the kingdom of God. You will have more fun and fulfillment in living in the kingdom of grace than you can imagine.

Points To Ponder

1. *Hate* in the back-side context of our parable (Luke 14:26) comes from the Greek word *miséo*. *Miséo* literally means "loving far less." See Luke 16:13 where the same concept is used to compare money to God.

2. *Only the lost listen* can be a confusing phrase. To understand it, we must understand that according to the Bible we are all lost until we are rescued by grace. Grace gives rise to repentance which means turning back to God. In terms of salvation, you don't turn back unless you know that you are going in the wrong direction. You don't turn back unless you know that you are lost.

3. *Grace*. Justice means getting what you deserve. Mercy means not getting what you deserve. Grace means getting what you do not deserve. This is a parable about grace.

Questions For Personal Consideration And/Or Group Discussion

1. Try to describe heaven.

2. According to the Bible, what do you need to do to go to heaven?

3. What do the guests at the Great Banquet have in common?

4. Comment on this statement, "When you compare yourself to God you are a bum."

5. What does the statement in the **Points To Ponder** about justice, mercy, and grace mean? Do you agree with the statement?

See **Digging Deeper**, p. 163, for further insights and application.

70

Chapter Eight

Wake Up!

Matthew 25:14-30

When I was a boy growing up in Chicago, I heard a song that has stuck with me all of my life. If you are sixty years old or older, you may remember it. It went something like this:

> *It's what ya' do with what ya' got*
> *And never mind how much ya' got*
> *It's what you do with what ya' got*
> *That pays off in the end.*

That is what the parable of the talents in Matthew 25:14-30 is all about. As a matter of fact, that is what all three stories in Matthew 25 are all about.

Three Stories

The first story (Matthew 25:1-13) is about the ten virgins, only half of whom were awake to the reality of the coming of the bridegroom. The wise virgins lit their lamps in preparation for the coming of the bridegroom. The five foolish virgins arose from their sleep, but were not ready when the bridegroom arrived. In other words, they did not trust the promise of God that he was coming back. They did not trust his word. We are called to believe in Christ now and trust his promise that he will return again.

First and foremost, we must have faith *in* God before we get to the question of using our talents *for* God. Once we believe, then we need to use what we have been given to light up the world before it is too late. It is what you do with what you've got that pays off in the end.

The second story (Matthew 25:14-30) is the parable of the talents. A wealthy Master (God) goes away on a trip, promising to come back soon. He entrusts talents to his stewards. Stewards are those who are temporarily in charge of what God owns. In Jesus' time a talent was a weight for measuring silver and gold. For our purposes today, let's say that one talent is about $1,000, two talents about $2,000, and five talents about $5,000. In other words, this is a parable about how we use, or don't use, our money for God.

As in the first parable, the first question is: "Do we believe in the Master and do we trust his promise that he is coming back soon?" The parable is about investment, not in the stock market, but in the kingdom of God. The five-talent man and the two-talent man both double what they have been given. The one-talent man buries his money. He does not understand the Master. He practices a "no investment, no return" policy. The sharp point of the parable is that what you don't use for God, you lose. It's not how much you've got, but what you do with what you've got that pays off in the end.

The third story (Matthew 25:31-46) is the story of judgment at the end of the world where the King of the universe divides those who are going to heaven from those who are going to hell. The King says, "Whatever you did for one of the least of these brothers of mine, you did for me" (Matthew 25:40). "Whatever you did not do for on one of the least of these, you did not do for me" (Matthew 25:45). In other words, the King of the universe is watching how you treat other people. What you do with what you've got will make an eternal difference when you die.

All three stories are about waking up to the reality of God and ordering your life accordingly.

Wake Up Now! Tomorrow Is Too Late

"Wake up!" That is the first thing Jesus said as he started his ministry. According to Mark 1:15 when Jesus went to Galilee to begin his preaching, the very first thing he said was, "The time has come. The kingdom of God is near. Repent and believe the good news." All three of the stories in Matthew 25 are about this theme of waking up to God and his ways.

72

Some years ago I was out of town on a speaking engagement. I had stayed up late the night before talking to the people from the convention I had addressed. Since I had to catch a plane early the next morning, I left a wake up call with the front desk. At 5:30 a.m. sharp, my telephone rang. I was so sleepy that I could hardly drag myself out of bed. I did not know who I was, where I was, or what I was supposed to do. When I finally got to the phone, the sweet voice of a young lady said, "This is your wake up call. Arise. Shine."

That is what is happening when Jesus says, "The time has come. The kingdom of God is at hand." That is what is happening in all three stories in Matthew 25. God is saying, "This is your wake up call. Arise. Let your good works shine." That is also what is happening every time we pray the Lord's Prayer.

Jesus gave the Lord's Prayer as a wake up call for his disciples. The Lord's Prayer is all about the kingdom of God and the need to live now in anticipation of the ultimate coming of God. The petition of the Lord's Prayer that says, "Thy kingdom come," says it best.

Christians are called to live as if the kingdom of God has already arrived. Of course the kingdom will not come in fullness until the end of time, but with the first coming of Jesus that kingdom is launched. Between the first and second coming of Jesus there is such a short span of time that his disciples are expected to live as if the kingdom has already arrived. That is why Jesus says, "The time has come. The kingdom of God is near." It may be years or even hundreds of years before the second coming of Christ, but we are called to live as if the span of time between the first and second coming is a very short period of time.

When I was a boy, my mother told me about the lightning and the thunder. "When you see the lightning, Ron, you know that the thunder will come soon. Count the seconds before the thunder follows the lightning and you will know how many miles away the lightning has struck." I don't know how accurate the seconds and the miles are scientifically. I do know that the one thing follows the other in what seems like no time at all. That is precisely what happens between the first and second coming of our Lord. When you see the coming of Jesus with the good news, it is no time at all before he will appear at the end of time and you will see him again in judgment.

Most people today seem to be living as if there is no God, no heaven or hell, and no judgment. The biblical corrective for careless, immoral, materialistic living is the wake up call: "The time has come. The kingdom is near. It is time to get up. Rise and let your light shine. Now."

It's What You Do With What You've Got
And Never Mind How Much You've Got ...

Gert Behanna lived the first sixty-some years of her life with more money than she knew how to spend. In the things of this world, she was not rich; she was filthy rich. But as to spiritual values, she was poor. She lived as if there was no God. Nobody told her about God. Nobody told her about the gospel of Jesus Christ. Nobody took her to church or taught her the Lord's Prayer. Gert was a thoroughly secular person. She had everything; yet she had nothing. Her money did not make her happy.

Gert's mother was beautiful. Gert was ugly. When she was a little girl, people would say to her mother, "Well, she is wholesome anyway." Later Gert remarked, "We women want to be pretty, 'man-killers,' or 'show-stoppers.' To call a woman of any age 'wholesome' is a great insult."

Gert's father was brilliant, successful, and very rich. He expected her to follow his example. Although her father sent her to the prestigious Sorbonne in France and expected her to find the cure for cancer, Gert failed to come close to the standards that were held up in front of her. She never even finished college. She was neither beautiful nor smart. On top of that, she failed at three marriages and was in serious personal trouble as an alcoholic and drug user.

She tried suicide. She took an overdose of pills that would have killed a horse, but she woke up in a California hospital with all kinds of tubes coming into her and going out of her. She had failed at everything else. Now she had failed at taking her own life. When she had sufficiently recovered to talk to a doctor, he said, "You are in very serious trouble with your health, but there is nothing wrong with you. I am going to send you to a psychiatrist."

"I don't need a psychiatrist; I need God," she responded. "I don't know where that statement came from," she said later. "I didn't mean it, but I said it."

When she got home to Chicago, she received an invitation from a friend to meet some very special people. "Who are they?" she asked. "They are Christians, Gert," her friend told her. "They used to have the same kind of problems with alcohol and drugs that you have." This was not acceptable social behavior with the very rich, but Gert went to her friend's house to meet these special people. To meet her first Christians she got drunk. Later she said, "That is not a comment on us drunks so much as it is a comment on us Christians!"

She was drunk. They were kind. She blamed her parents and her three husbands for all her troubles. They said, "You do have problems, Gert. Why don't you turn them over to God?"

"You mean turn my problems over to God like I turn my luggage over to a porter?"

"Yes, something like that," they said.

These two Christians did not correct her theology. They let her have God as a porter. They encouraged her to believe. They not only said it. They meant it. When something is meant, it can make a difference.

When she got home from visiting her first Christians, she found a note from them. "Welcome home, Gert. We are praying for you every day. Enclosed find an article on 'How to Become a Christian' by Sam Shoemaker. We hope that you will read it."

She read it and everything changed. "It is hard to describe. It is more like stepping into a shower covered with dirt and coming out clean than anything else with which I could compare it," Gert said. "One minute I was filled with resentments, anger, and hatred. The next I was a Christian. I fell to my knees and tried to think of a prayer. From somewhere deep in my subconscious mind emerged these words, 'Our Father.'" Somewhere she had heard these words of the Lord's Prayer.

"If God is my Father," she thought, "then all the people in the world are my brothers and sisters." Thus began the career of one of the greatest speakers for God in the twentieth century. She gave away most of her money to the church. She wanted everyone else

75

to meet her heavenly Father. The kingdom of God had broken into her life. She woke up and acted on her new-found faith in Christ.

That is what Jesus is talking about in Matthew 25. That is what he means by urging us to use our talents for other people.

Waking up and finding saving faith in Jesus Christ is the first step. The second is to do something beautiful with your life. Don't squander life. It is precious. Don't use your time simply to gain the things of this world. Things rust away and don't mean anything in the end. In the words of Mother Teresa of Calcutta, India, "Do something beautiful for God."

In the parable of the talents, Jesus is warning us that since we live today between the lightning and the thunder, we need to use the gifts he has given us to help people find meaning and purpose by finding God. We need to bless others as we have been blessed. "As you have done it to the least of my brothers and sisters," Jesus said, "you have done it to me."

There was a successful business man in New York City who had recently become a Christian. He had turned his life over to Jesus Christ. He wanted to improve his behavior, to be more Christ-like. As he was shaving one morning, he prayed, "Lord, it was easier to become a Christian than to live as a Christian. I have given my life to you, but I feel that I am not living up to what you want me to be. Today, please put someone in my way so that I can help him see what you are like."

This business man rushed down to the train station to catch his train to work. He was running late, so when the conductor yelled, "All aboard," he rushed toward the door of the train. Just then he bumped something. It was a little boy. The puzzle that the boy had held in his hand was scattered all over the platform. "Sorry, son," the man said, and started running for his train again. Then suddenly he stopped. He walked back to where the boy was sitting on the platform crying and trying to put the puzzle pieces back in the box. Methodically the man picked up the pieces of the puzzle and placed them in the box. "There, son. I'm really sorry that I bumped you," he said as the train pulled away.

"Mister," said the boy.

"Yes."

"Are you Jesus?"

It's not how much you've got, but what you do with what you've got that pays off in the end.

Points To Ponder

1. *A talent* (Matthew 25:15) was not a coin. It was a weight. Its value depended on whether the coinage was copper, gold, or silver. Some scholars estimate the value of the talent in our story at over $1,000.

2. *Differing gifts.* Everyone does not have the same gifts. Some are given more, some less. What matters is not how many gifts you have, but how you use what God has given you.

3. *The servant who was punished in our story* is the one who doesn't try. He is afraid to risk what he has been given and thus loses his one talent. The only way to keep a gift from God is to use it. In sports, it is often said, "Use it, or lose it."

Questions For Personal Consideration And/Or Group Discussion

1. What do you do when you see warning signs on the highway?

2. How are the parables in Matthew 25 warning signs of what is up ahead?

3. What difference would it make if we heeded the warnings in these three parables?

See **Digging Deeper**, p. 164, for further insights and applications.

Section Two:

Kingdom Invitations

Chapter Nine

Punctured Misconceptions About The Lost And Found

Luke 15:1-32

Recently, someone asked me where the lost and found department was at our church. I replied, "We don't have a lost and found department at church. You might try the secretary's desk. Sometimes people leave things that are lost and found there. What did you lose?"

"I lost a pair of prescription glasses," the member said. "I can't see well without them."

A few days later I realized my misconception. The whole church is a lost and found department. My misconception was popped as I read Luke 15:1-31. The story starts out with murmuring by spiritually blind Pharisees and religious teachers and ends up with an elder brother murmuring outside the party for his younger brother who has returned from the far country where he was lost.

Murmuring is a sign that you are more lost than sinful people like the tax collectors in Luke 15:1-3. Murmuring shows that you are more lost than the disoriented, lost sheep in Luke 15:4-7, more lost than the misplaced coin in Luke 15:8-10, and more lost than the younger son in Luke 15:11-31. Murmuring is a sign that you cannot see the values of the kingdom of God.

Lost, Sinful People

The tax collectors in Jesus' time were Jews who had sold out to Rome. The Romans had conquered the ancient world. Tax collectors raised money for the Romans by squeezing as much as they could from the conquered people. The tax collectors were not paid a salary, but they could keep any money they raised beyond what the Romans demanded. They were viewed by the Jews as the worst of sinners because they were traitors to the Jewish nation and because they were scoundrels who got rich off the profits of left over taxes from the people. They were considered the sinful scum of society.

In order to understand the scandal of Jesus talking to and including the tax collectors in his ministry, try to imagine Jesus spending time with Mafia leaders or leaders of drug cartels. These notorious sinners are hated today just as the tax collectors were hated in Jesus' day. Our general attitude about Mafia leaders or leaders of drug cartels is, "Lock them up and throw away the key." Some notorious sinners are just plain evil, aren't they? Some are so evil that they are beyond reach, aren't they?

Jesus teaches that nobody is beyond the reach of God except those who refuse to listen and repent for their sins. Those who murmur against people they consider below them are not listening to God and repenting of their own sins.

Murmuring is the sound that comes from people who think that they are bigger and better than they really are. Murmuring is the sound that comes when people who look down on other people. Murmuring comes from judgmental and self-righteous people. Murmuring against others is both understandable and dangerous. It is understandable because we all struggle against being judgmental. It is dangerous because it can send you to hell.

Recently I heard murmuring in a barber shop. The barbers were murmuring against a homeless man who was dressed in tattered clothes. "He is irresponsible," one said. "He is a bum," another chimed in. "He is a drag on society," a third responded. You have heard murmuring in barber shops, beauty parlors, at work, at home, about family members, and friends. You have probably also heard murmuring in churches. Most people who murmur don't realize how much the Bible speaks out against the dangers of murmuring.

The Israelites' murmurings against Moses and God in the wilderness are severely punished. Most of the parables of Jesus, including this one, are set up by self-righteous murmuring. It is not that we are expected to refrain from making judgments. We must

82

make judgments about people in order to stay away from evil, in order to follow the good, and in business in order to hire productive people and fire unproductive people. Murmuring is different than making judgments. We must always be careful and prayerful about making judgments, but murmuring goes beyond making judgments in the every day world of decision making. Murmuring means being judgmental. Jesus makes judgments without falling into the pit of being judgmental.

Jesus makes a judgment that the Pharisees and religious teachers are the notorious sinners. He also makes the judgment that some of the tax collectors can be reached. In Luke 5:27-32, Jesus calls Levi, a tax collector, to follow him. Levi becomes Matthew, the apostle. When he is criticized for his action, Jesus says, "It is not the healthy who need a doctor, but the sick. I have not come to call the righteous (read self-righteous), but sinners to repentance." Pop! There goes a misconception.

Jesus came to call sinners. He also came to call the disoriented.

Lost, Disoriented People

The lost sheep in Luke 15:4-7 get disoriented when they leave the flock. They are not evil, just not very smart. Sheep cannot live very long unless they stay together with other sheep. If they wander off, the wolves will get them. If wolves attack the flock, the shepherd uses his baseball-bat-like rod to beat them off. The shepherd uses his staff to hit the sheep on the backside to keep them from going astray and getting into danger.

If a sheep wanders off, the good shepherd leaves the flock and goes off to find the disoriented sheep. If the shepherd finds the lost sheep on the shelf of a mountain where it has fallen, he uses the crook of the staff to reach down to the shelf and rescue the sheep.

Some people are like the lost, disoriented sheep in the parable. They leave the flock, the church, wander among the wolves of the world, and get hurt or killed. Jesus saw Levi not only as a notorious sinner, but as a disoriented son who had foolishly separated from the faithful. That is why he invited him to follow him.

Later Matthew, a disciple, reports in his Gospel that Jesus saw children as disoriented and neglected too. Children were regarded as property in Jesus' day. They were seen as unimportant. They were looked down upon. Jesus viewed them differently. "See that you do not look down on one of these little ones. For I tell you that their angels in heaven always see the face of my Father in heaven. What do you think? If a man owns a hundred sheep, and one of them wanders away, will he not leave the ninety-nine on the hills and go to look for the one that wandered off? And if he finds it, I tell you the truth, he is happier about that one sheep than about the ninety-nine that did not wander off. In the same way your Father in heaven is not willing that any of these little ones should be lost" (Matthew 18:10-14). Pop! There goes another misconception.

Lost, Misplaced People

The misplaced coin story in Luke 15:8-10 has the same theme as the lost sheep story. The Father is diligent in his search for his lost children.

In Israel, a poor housewife who lost a coin would diligently look for it because she needed it for her family's welfare. She needed it for food, clothing, and shelter. Even though a coin is small, it is important to a poor woman. Even though rich and powerful people might just forget about it, she didn't. The smallest coin meant a lot to her.

There are many people who are small and seemingly unimportant. There are many who seem to have little value in the eyes of the world. They easily get misplaced and forgotten as the wheels of progress grind away. God never forgets them. God seeks them out, finds them, and holds them up as examples to all of us.

In Mark 12:41-44 Jesus tells the story of a widow who made a cameo appearance at the Temple treasury one day. She put in two very small copper coins. Jesus said, "I tell you the truth, this poor widow has put more into the treasury than all the others. They all gave out of their wealth; but she, out of her poverty, put in everything — all she had to live on" (Mark 12:43-44).

The seemingly misplaced, unimportant widow is a heroine in God's sight. Jesus holds her up for us to see like a shiny new coin found by the woman in the parable. What the widow did is real stewardship, not giving leftovers like so many do. "You who have eyes to see, come and behold what I have found," Jesus says. Pop! There goes still another misconception.

Lost, Different People

There are many angles from which to see the many truths of the parable of the prodigal son (Luke 15:11-31). We will examine many of these in the next two chapters. Here we will look at the younger son who is not only lost, but is different from his older brother.

The two sons are really different. The elder son is responsible; the younger son irresponsible. The elder son is a diligent, hard worker; the younger son a devil-may-care no-account who runs off with his inheritance and spends it on wine, women, and song. The elder son is careful; the younger son careless. The elder son is obedient; the younger son disobedient. We expect Jesus to compliment the one and condemn the other. Pop! There goes another misconception.

The elder son seemingly does everything right and only one little thing wrong. His virtues have been noted. He is responsible, hard working, careful, and obedient. Are we to put these virtues aside as if they are not important? No, that's not the point of the parable at all. When we consider a parable, we should always look for one simple yet profound point. Parables are not moral example stories. They are stories intended to pop our misconceptions. The misconception of what is really dangerous to our spiritual health comes to light as we look at the one thing wrong in the personality of the older son.

The father in the parable invites the elder son to come to the party, but he refuses. He is caught in a trap of his own making. A judgmental attitude is vented in murmuring. Look at him there, out by the barn. Listen. "All these years I have been slaving for you ... But when this son of yours who has squandered your property with prostitutes comes home, you kill the fattened calf for him!"

At the end of Luke 15, the elder son is out by the barn murmuring against his brother and his father, just as the Pharisees at the beginning of Luke 15 are murmuring against Jesus and his treatment of sinners.

85

Oops! There goes the biggest misconception of all. Murmuring, which seems minor compared to the really big sins, can keep you out of the party called the kingdom of God.

Points To Ponder

1. *The Pharisees* were one of three chief Jewish parties in the time of Jesus. The other two parties were the Sadducees and the Essenes. Originally, the Pharisees were a reform party of men of strong religious character who reacted to the tendency of the Jews of their time to adopt the practices of Greek customs. By the time of Jesus, Pharisaism had become little more than an inherited belief for many of the participants. Unlike the Sadducees, the doctrines of the Pharisees included the resurrection of the body. In that respect, they agreed with Jesus, but unlike Jesus they taught that men are rewarded in the afterlife for conformity to the Law and that the disposition of the heart was less important than outward acts of obedience to the Law. They believed that the promises of God's grace are for the doers of the Law. John the Baptist called the Pharisees a generation of vipers. Jesus denounced them for their self-righteousness, their hypocrisy, and their cunning (Matthew 5:20; 16:6, 11, 12; and 23:1-39). Here in Luke 15:1-2, Jesus denounced them for murmuring. Before his conversion to Christianity, Paul was a Pharisee who had been taught by Gamaliel (Acts 5:34). The Pharisees did many good things, but often for the wrong reason. T. S. Eliot, the poet, once wrote words that describe the Pharisees well: "The last temptation is the greatest treason, / To do the right thing for the wrong reason."

2. *The Scribes* were copiers and teachers of the Law. Some of the Scribes were members of the Sanhedrin, the Jewish Supreme Court. Some were followers of Jesus (Matthew 8:19), but most found fault with him and murmured against him.

3. *The muttering or murmuring* of the Pharisees and Scribes is what gave rise to Jesus' parables in Luke 15.

Questions For Personal Consideration
And/Or Group Discussion

1. What kinds of things do self-righteous people say about others?

2. If you are in a group that is talking about someone in a derogatory way, and you speak up for that person, what generally happens?

3. In his interpretation of the eighth commandment, Luther says that we should always put the most charitable interpretation on our neighbor's behavior. How does that play out in real life?

See **Digging Deeper**, p. 165, for further insights and applications.

Chapter Ten

The Predicament
Of The Loving Father

Luke 15:11-32

The focus of this story seems to be the prodigal son. The younger son was not appreciative of his father's house. He demanded that he be given his inheritance. He blew his money in the big city. He ran out of money and had to get a job. He repented. He came home. The focus of Luke 15:11-32 appears to be the wayward son. That is why this parable is generally named the parable of the prodigal son. But this apparent focus is an illusion. The real focus is the waiting father.

The father's heart makes the return possible. Grace and generosity and the father's incredible willingness to forgive are all in the spotlight as we consider this story.

Jesus, who told this story, was a Jew. In Hebrew thinking, God, not man, is always central. The prodigal son only appears to be the protagonist of this dramatic story. In fact, he is only one of the people in the supporting cast. We will start by looking at the supporting cast, but we will move toward the central theme of the father and the predicament in which he finds himself in Luke 15:11-32.

Supporting Cast: Prodigal And Semi-Prodigal
Sons And Daughters

The prodigal son is only one of the members of the supporting cast in this story. We are in this cast of characters as well. Most Christians rank the so-called parable of the prodigal son right up there at the top of the list of favorite Bible stories, but many people keep the pricking, pinching, prodding aspects of this story at a distance by thinking that it is a story about someone else.

Helmut Thielicke tells the story of his young son sitting down in front of a large mirror. At first the boy does not recognize himself because he is too young. He enjoys seeing the small image from the mirror, but that is all he sees. Then, all of a sudden, the expression on his face changes as he begins to recognize the similarity of motions in the mirror to his own motions. He seems to be saying, "That's me."[6]

That is what can happen when we read or hear this story. "That's me," we can say, recognizing that in some strange, mysterious way, this is our story. We may not have done the extreme things done by the younger son, but in many ways we can identify with him.

Wes Seeliger suggests that most church members can get into this story if they think of themselves as "semi-prodigals." He says, "We semi-prodigals play both ends against the middle. We want to live on our own without burning our bridges behind us. We keep in touch, just in case. We steer clear of both our father's house and the pig pen. We avoid both the radical demand and the wild promise of the father's love."[7]

As we read or hear this story, whether we say, "That's me," or "I'm one of the semi-prodigals," we are in the story as supporting cast members. It will help us get into the story if we look for ourselves as participants, not outsiders observing someone else's behavior. It may also help us to get into the story as participants by looking at the story in a somewhat different setting.

In order to get into the mind-set of the prodigal, let me frame the story in a modern setting. In the wine country of northern California, there is a vineyard owned by a man with two sons. One day, over a bowl of Wheaties, the younger son says to his father, "I am tired of this place. I am tired of this hard work. I am tired of responsibility. I want out. I want what is coming to me."

His father is saddened by the young man's dissatisfaction and demands, but he decides to give his son his share of the inheritance and his freedom. That is part of the father's predicament. Should he try to hold onto the boy and keep him from danger, or let go and take a chance of never seeing him again? He decides to let him go. What a sad day it is when the father says, "Goodbye," to his youngest son.

The young man goes off to San Francisco. He has never seen the big city before. He has money in his pockets and freedom in his heart. He buys a new red sports car. He frequents many bars and meets all kinds of people, including some prostitutes. He doesn't need much encouragement to "sow his wild oats."

When he comes into his favorite bar, people come up and greet him because he always buys drinks. After a few drinks, the young man starts to boast, as is his custom. People in bars often boast when they drink too much. He blames other people for his troubles, as people often do in bars. Ask any bartender. The young man's drinking partners only half-listen to his tales. When the free drinks stop, the so-called friends stop listening.

The time comes when the young man runs out of money. He has to sell his sports car. When that money runs out, he thinks, "My friends will take care of me." They don't. Finally, he decides to get a job. A farmer on the outskirts of San Francisco hires him.

"How about a little advance?" the young man asks.

"Payday is Friday," says the stern farmer.

As the young man slops the hogs, he is at an all-time low. He is Jewish. Jews avoid eating pork. The young man realizes that he has hit bottom. Then something happens that changes the course of his life.

The Bible says that "he comes to his senses" (Luke 15:17). Another translation reads, "He came to himself" (RSV). He is hungry and broke. He remembers home. He remembers his father. He thinks, "Even the servants in my father's house eat better than I am eating."

As soon as payday comes, the boy hitchhikes his way toward home. He practices his speech every chance he gets. "Father, I have sinned against heaven and against you. I am no longer worthy to be called your son; make me like one of your hired men." As he gets out of the car that had picked him up as a hitchhiker, he looks at the familiar surroundings of the road leading to the family vineyard. He is scared. He looks at the magnificent sunset and thinks,

91

"You worthless bum. You blew it. What makes you think that your father will want you back under any circumstances?"

He tries to straighten up his clothes, but that does not help much since the clothes are very dirty from sleeping out of doors. He pulls up his belt, straightens his hat, picks up a handful of stones, and throws them at bushes along the familiar dusty road. He walks over the little hills and down into the valleys where he had played as a child, meditating on the hundreds of close calls he has had in the last several months. Twice he was rolled and robbed by prostitutes. He found himself sleeping in the gutter more than once. "I am not worthy," he says out loud.

Two blocks from home, the young man sees the door of his home come flying open. He freezes.

The Predicament Of The Loving Father

Someone comes running toward the young man. It is his father. Where can he hide? What can he say? What was that speech he had practiced all the way home? "Father, I have sinned ... I am no longer worthy...." He can't get the words out. The father interrupts him, saying to the servants who had run out with him, "Quick! Bring the best robe and put it on him. Put a ring on his finger and sandals on his feet" (Luke 15:22). The sandals and clothes are a total shock. The ring is a greater shock. That's the ring of ownership. His father is fully restoring him to the family. A more sensible approach would be to give the young man a year or two to prove himself, but no, this father is motivated by something beyond common sense. This father, like the heavenly father, is primarily motivated by extravagant grace.

The young man is speechless. As we read this story, we are speechless. This is shocking behavior. The father gobbles the young man up in his arms, saying, "My son. My son. My son has come home." To the servants he says, "Let's have a party. Bring the fattened calf and kill it. Let's have a feast and celebrate. For this son of mine was dead and is alive again; he was lost and is found."

"But, Father, I have sinned ..." the young man stammers. "I don't deserve anything. I was just hoping that I might be like a hired hand."

"Yes, I know," says the father, "but you are my son. Welcome home."

This is your story and mine. It is a story about misused freedom and broken relationships in families. It is a story about heartbreak and apparent hopelessness. It is a story about prodigals and semi-prodigals. It is a story about coming home. It is a story about justice and mercy, but mostly it is a story about God and his grace.

Justice means that I get what I deserve. The young man expects to hear, "I told you so." Justice means punishment of evil deeds. Justice is at play in the story because justice is at play in the heart of God. The predicament of the loving father is that he knows that the son deserves punishment. But justice is not the primary motivation of the father's heart. Justice is not the theme of this story.

Mercy means that I do not get what I deserve. Mercy is at play in the story. The young man is shocked that he is not getting what he deserves. He is shocked by the mercy of his father. Mercy is at the heart of God, but not even mercy is the primary theme of this story.

Grace means that I get what I do not deserve. The grace of God is the heart of this story. Grace overcomes justice and goes beyond mercy. The predicament of the loving father is that while justice and mercy are a part of his nature, when repentance is involved, even inadequate stammering repentance, amazing grace pushes its way through and reveals what God is really like.

Theologian James Kallas tells the story of how he preached his first sermon on this parable. He was a seminarian at the time. He was assigned to preach at a little country church. He was so keyed up about the assignment that he spent hundreds of hours working on the manuscript. The Saturday night before he was to preach, he could hardly sleep. He awoke early Sunday morning and said to his wife, "Let's go."

"Are you crazy?" she replied. "It's 4 a.m."

"I know," Kallas said, "but I don't want to be late."

The seminarian, his wife, and newborn son arrived at the empty church two hours early. That left enough time to practice and re-practice the sermon he had prepared. Finally 9 a.m. arrived. Only two people showed up.

"What do we do?" the disappointed seminarian asked the usher. "We will have service anyway," the usher replied.

For almost an hour, James Kallas dumped the whole load on the two parishioners, his wife, and his newborn son. He waxed eloquent about the prodigal and his problems, his sins, and his errors in judgment.

A more mature James Kallas said, "There was a serious flaw in my first sermon. My son was given ample and strong reasons to forever avoid prodigality, but I missed the point of the parable. The parable is not primarily about the prodigal son. The parable is about God."

The point of the parable is that God is waiting for all of us to come home. His arms are outstretched. His heart is open. His grace goes out to meet us long before we repent.

If you are a prodigal or just a semi-prodigal, this story is for you. If you are morally libertine or just a little self-centered, this story is for you. If you are a church member who attends church regularly or someone who has not darkened the door of a church for years, this story is for you. There is only one way into heaven. The way is forgiveness. Forgiveness is only possible because grace is in the heart of the loving father. The Father is waiting for you to come home.

Do you remember who you are? Will you come to your senses? Will you come to yourself?

The door is open. Will you come home? Will you come to the party?

If you start for home, even for some wrong reasons, you will find this door open. If you remember what the Father is like, you will discover that he is better than you have ever imagined. If you discover that you are in this story, and say, "That's me!" you will discover or re-discover the amazing grace of God and the kingdom of God.

Points To Ponder

1. *Slopping hogs* is the lowest status of all for Jews. It was strictly forbidden for Jews. The law said, "Cursed is he who feeds swine."[8] In ancient times, pork was forbidden because there was no refrigeration and pork spoiled easily. The Jews have maintained their identity over the years as a people who do not eat pork.

2. *The inheritance.* In Jewish practice, the eldest son usually got two-thirds of the inheritance; the younger son one-third. See Deuteronomy 21:17. There were two ways to divide the property: 1) by a will and 2) by a gift during the life of the father. The problem of the younger son's request of a gift was the harshness of the demand. For a more thorough discussion of Jewish inheritance, see William Barclay's commentary on *The Gospel of Luke* (Westminster Press, Philadelphia, 1975, p. 204) or Joachim Jeremias' book *The Parables Of Jesus* (Charles Scribner's Sons, New York, 6th edition, 1962, pp. 128 and 129).

3. *Not fully yourself.* This parable shows that a person is not fully himself until he heads for home with the father. The homecoming of the younger son did not result in his being a slave in his father's house as he expected. Instead, he was finally free to be himself. On the other hand, the elder son, while physically free, was not fully himself and therefore a slave to wrong ideas about his father. The Pharisees and Scribes in verses one and two were like him in this respect. They, like the elder son, could still come to the kingdom party if they would only repent of their short-sightedness about God. To repent and come home means to discover who you are. Saint Paul describes evangelism in terms of helping people come to their full maturity in Christ. "We proclaim him, admonishing and teaching everyone with all wisdom, so that we may present everyone perfect (mature, whole, complete) in Christ" (Colossians 1:28).

4. *Consider this parable in the light of Baptism.* Baptism makes us children of the loving Father. We are his children whether we do his work or not. We are his children whether we stay at home or wander off to sinful places. We are his children whether we are good or bad. But if we wander away from the Father, and thus break his heart, we are lost children. When we repent and come home, we re-discover that we are welcomed home by the grace of God. The grace of God comes before repentance and follows after repentance. We are baptized into the grace of God when we are children and have not yet learned to repent. When we finally wake up and start back home, our repentance may not be altogether honorable and is certainly inadequate, but even a slight turning back brings us the benefits of grace.

5. *Appropriating what has been accomplished.* The prodigal son appropriated what God has accomplished. God does what is necessary for us to be forgiven. Jesus died on the cross for all people everywhere. From the cross Jesus said, "It is finished." The work of salvation has been accomplished. The problem is that most people do not know what this means. Our job is not to accomplish salvation. Our job is to appropriate what has already been accomplished. Salvation is a gift of grace. God has written the check for a million dollars. Our names are on that check. All we have to do is endorse what has already been given. Endorsing what has been given is called repentance. The younger son's "coming to himself" is that turn toward home called repentance. He only turned toward home because he remembered, however inadequately, that his father had a loving heart. Grace comes before and follows after the turn toward home.

6. *Holy Communion* is God's forgiveness party for his returning sons and daughters. Holy Communion is a foretaste of the kingdom of God banquet that God has prepared for us. As undeserving sinners we mysteriously receive the grace of God in,

through, and under the bread and wine. We know that we receive Christ in the elements because Christ promised that it would be so. God never breaks a promise. Faith appropriates what grace has accomplished for us on the cross. "But we are not worthy, Father," we protest. The Father replies, "Yes, I know, but come to my banquet anyway."

Questions For Personal Consideration And/Or Group Discussion

1. Do you like or not like the term "semi-prodigals"?

2. How does this parable fit family situations you know about?

3. Is grace really a practical motivation for our behavior toward other people?

See **Digging Deeper**, p. 166, for further insights and applications.

Chapter Eleven

The Predicament
Of The Elder Son

Luke 15:1-2, 11-32

In the last chapter we focused on God the Father, the main character in the parable that we so often call the parable of the prodigal son. We also looked at the cast of other characters in this story, including ourselves. Here in this chapter we will look at the elder son. Many of us find ourselves in the first part of the story. If we look closely, we may find ourselves in this part of the story as well.

The younger son did almost everything wrong and only one thing right. He came home. The elder son did almost everything right and only one thing wrong. He refused to come home. The door of the father's house stood wide open. The father invited the elder son to come in. He refused to come home. The elder son refused to come home to the party for his younger brother, the philanderer. Instead, he murmured, "That son of yours...."

Isn't the elder son justified in his judgment? Doesn't he have a right to complain? Don't good work habits count for anything? Where would the world be if we did not have hard-working, responsible people who carried more than their share? Don't people like the elder son keep the world from falling apart? What's the problem here?

Good questions. It may help to keep three things in mind as we look at this story. First, we must remember that Jesus is Jewish. As noted earlier, in Hebrew thinking, God, not man, is the center. This is a story about God, not a story about how people succeed or fail in business.

Second, this is a story about the kingdom of God, not the kingdoms of the world. This is also a story about religious misconceptions. Something that may be valid by worldly standards may not apply to the kingdom of God. That is why parables about the kingdom of God shock us. They are supposed to shock us. The kingdom of God operates on different principles than the kingdoms of this world.

Third, as I noted in chapter 9, the real problem Jesus is attacking in the fifteenth chapter of Luke is murmuring and the attitude of superiority and judgment in the Pharisees and Scribes (Luke 15:1-2). The elder son is angry, resentful, and jealous when a party is thrown for a sinner who comes home. At the end of the parable, he is still standing outside the party, murmuring to himself.

With those three points in mind, let's look deeper at the responsible elder son in the story of the waiting father.

The Responsible Elder Son

The elder son is responsible. Being responsible often results in success. Those who study birth order tell us that eldest and only children tend to be responsible and therefore successful by worldly standards. A disproportionately high percent of presidents, senior pastors, astronauts, and business leaders are firstborn or only children. Of course, middle or last children can be successful as well, but it is interesting that the villain in our story is a successful, elder son.

The elder son stays on the farm and works hard. Doesn't that count for anything? Doesn't a conservative work ethic and saving one's money mean anything? From what little we know, the elder son appears to be a faithful church member, a model citizen, and a dependable manager. Does the father ignore all this proper behavior?

Why turn the house upside down for a no-account brother who will probably leave again in a few days or weeks after squeezing a few more dollars out of the old man? Has he really changed? Why not give him a two-year probation period? If he passes that test, then we can celebrate. Is not coming to a party for a no-good, irresponsible brother all that bad? Why all this fuss about him when you have never thrown a party like this for me? These are responsible questions and thoughts that may have been in the mind of the elder son.

The Pharisees and Scribes to whom this parable was addressed must have had the same questions. We keep the religious rules, don't we? We go to the synagogue or Temple regularly, don't we? We tithe, read our Bibles, and pray, don't we? What's so terrible?

What's so terrible is that the Pharisees and Scribes and their parable counterpart, the elder son, take God for granted. They fall into what today is called "cultural Christianity." Cultural Christians agree to the doctrines of the faith and try to follow the morals of the faith, but lack a living relationship with the heavenly Father. Caught up in many good things, they miss the most important thing of all. The most important thing of all is that we can come into the kingdom of God only through repentance and faith in Jesus Christ. Everything depends on God's grace, not our good works, if we are going to be children of the heavenly Father. As Saint Paul puts it, "For it is by grace you have been saved, through faith — and this not of yourselves, it is the gift of God — not by works, so that no one can boast" (Ephesians 2:8-9).

What's so terrible is that the elder son and his counterparts have forgotten the wonder of being loved and forgiven by the Father. Forgiveness, the pricking point of this parable, has become a banality for the elder son and his counterparts. They have forgotten that the only way to the Father is by grace.

What's so terrible is that the lack of understanding of God's grace is evident in the criticism and murmuring against sinners who return home to God by repentance. Nobody is so good that absolute judgment may be rendered on the repentance of others.

What's so terrible is that responsible people can fall into the trap of taking themselves too seriously. They can become so preoccupied with themselves that they neglect to come to the party.

I am an only child. Like many only children and firstborns, I tend to be responsible. It is easy to slip from being responsible to taking myself too seriously. It is also important for me to watch my tendency toward high closure. Quick decision-making can lead to being judgmental of others.

Bill and Sam, two senior pastors of large churches, were talking one day about decision-making and the problem of being judgmental. "Honestly," Bill said, "I think that sometimes you are judgmental toward other pastors."

"I think that you are judgmental too," Sam replied.

Bill's comeback is interesting. "You are judgmental. I am just high on closure," he replied.

Whether judgmental or just high on closure, responsible people must be careful about falling into the trap of the elder son in our story. Jealousy, resentment, and murmuring toward the apparently irresponsible people we meet may reveal more about us than them. In our personal behavior, we are all called to be more like the God of grace in the parable of the waiting father.

The Father Is Waiting For The Responsible Son As Well As The Younger Son To Come Home

That the father is waiting for the younger son to arrive home has been said so often that we expect it, even if we don't fully comprehend it. That the father is waiting for the responsible son to come home is less obvious, but no less true.

It is less obvious because the elder son is home already, at least physically. But is he really home? If he won't come to the repentance and forgiveness party, he may be living in the same house with the father, but he doesn't know the heart and love of the father.

This is the kingdom of God party for everyone: irresponsible prodigals and responsible workers, failures and people who have grand successes to their credit, poor people who don't know where their next meal will come from, and wealthy people who need not worry about having enough to eat all get into the kingdom of God by grace alone.

The problem with monetary and religious prosperity is that it tends to make us pompous. The father is inclusive enough for thousands of pompous elder sons if they will just repent and come to the party, but it is the pomposity and lack of repentance that keep them out. That was the problem of the Pharisees, Scribes, and the elder son.

Please note that Jesus preached to the Pharisees and Scribes, yet they did not come into his kingdom by faith. As a matter of fact, they refused to come. They were so inflated with themselves that they did not listen to the invitation.

Please note that the father comes out of the house with an invitation to the elder son to come to the party, just as he came out of the house with an invitation to the younger son. The father pleads for both of his children to come home. Luke 15:58 says that the father entreated the elder son to join the party. Verse 31 says that the father pleaded, "Son, it is fitting for you to come to the party for what has been lost has been found." The pleas fall on deaf ears.

In one of his fiction books, C. S. Lewis has God sending a bus to hell each year, inviting people to get on and visit heaven and consider staying. Surprisingly, hardly anyone makes the transfer. Why? Because people send themselves to hell and keep themselves there by their own unwillingness to repent and come home. "All day long I have held out my arms to a disobedient and gainsaying people, but you would not come," says the Lord.

The lack of willingness to acknowledge that you have been wrong is the deadly sin lifted up in this part of the parable of the waiting father. The lack of repentance is an unwillingness to come home on God's terms. This lack of repentance is not only *a* deadly sin. It is *the* deadly sin.

The unforgivable sin is not murder or adultery, as serious as these sins are. You can repent and be forgiven for them. The unforgivable sin is not stealing or lying, as hurtful as these are in human relationships. For these sins you can repent and be forgiven. The unforgivable sin is not idolatry, taking the name of God in vain, dishonoring parents, bearing false witness, or coveting things. You can repent and be forgiven for any or all of them. The unforgivable sin, called blasphemy against the Holy Spirit in Matthew 12:31, is not to repent.

When the father pleads, "Come home," and you refuse to come because to come home means to acknowledge that you have been wrong, you commit the unpardonable sin — not repenting. To refuse to acknowledge that you are not all you should be keeps you out of the banquet party. That was the predicament of the elder son, the Pharisees and the Scribes.

Murmuring against the generous forgiveness of God is a sign that you don't understand the most basic thing of all — forgiveness. God's generous grace is the only way that any of us get into the kingdom. God's generous grace is the only reason we can stay in the kingdom.

Every long-time church member, as well as every late-comer; every professor of theology, as well as every mentally handicapped believer; every rich man in the things of this world, as well as every pauper, gets into the kingdom of God in only this one way — God's amazing grace. That is the point of the parable of the waiting father.

The door is open. The younger son came in. The elder son did not.

Points To Ponder

1. *While the best title for this parable is the parable of the waiting father or the parable of the loving father, in a secondary way we might also call it the parable of the lost son.* A case can easily be made for the prodigal son being the lost son who came home. From the last part of the story, we could just as easily make the point that the elder son is the one who is lost since he never came into the party.

2. *Go back and ponder the three points in the introduction* to this chapter. The interpretation given to the parable here is based on these three foundations.

3. *Ponder Matthew 19:27-20 and 20:1-16.* Compare the elder son's attitude with that of the complaining (murmuring) laborers who worked hard all day and got the same pay as those who worked less hours.

4. *Ponder Ephesians 2:8-9.* The problem many responsible people easily fall into is boasting which does not leave room for grace.

5. *Ponder Colossians 1:28.* The problem with those who don't come to the banquet of God is that they are not fully themselves yet. They are not mature.

6. *Ponder Matthew 12:31* which is about blasphemy against the Holy Spirit.

Questions For Personal Consideration And/Or Group Discussion

1. When you were a child, did you ever feel that you were responsible and others were not or did you feel that you were not responsible and others were responsible?

2. Where do you fall in your family birth order? Are you a first-born child or an only child? Are you a middle child? Are you a last child? What difference does this make in the way you turned out?

3. What was the elder son's problem?

4. If you are in a group study of this chapter, have each member of the group murmur out loud for thirty seconds. Talk about the sound of murmuring.

See **Digging Deeper**, p. 167, for further insights and applications.

Chapter Twelve

Who Could Ask
For Anything More?

Matthew 19:27-30; 20:1-16

Marty Haugen once observed: "There are stories that cannot be silenced. There are stories that are stronger than death. There are stories that can raise us from our sins.'"[9] Can the parable of the laborers in the vineyard do all that? At first glance, this story does not seem to be a story that can do any of that.

At first glance, this story is quite confusing. It appears to be a maze with no way out. Jesus spoke these words and Christians want to believe them, but how can they be true? The landowner seems to have mixed-up values. The pay off at the end of this parable seems grossly unfair.

From the point of view of common sense, this parable appears to come to the wrong conclusion. It seems to be the opposite of the proper way to think. Instead of chiding those who complain about unjust wages, shouldn't Jesus be scolding the landowner for unjust labor practices?

If This Is A Parable About Labor Relations,
We Are In Deep Trouble

If Jesus is telling us how to run a business, we are in a dark room wrapped up in an enigma. Can you imagine running a business by paying the same amount to someone who works for eight hours and someone else who works for only one hour? Such behavior could easily result in a lawsuit. In a court of law, wouldn't the jury favor the person who worked eight hours and got the same pay as a person who worked just one hour? Of course he would. If you were on the jury, how would you vote?

Eugene Lowery describes the case for the person who started to work early and was underpaid like this: "This is a good case for the National Labor Relations Board, don't you think? In fact, I'm shocked. Why on earth would Jesus take the side of an unjust owner? In fact, you know, that business of paying last ones first ... that was cruel and it was dumb."[10]

The owner in our story forced the 7 a.m. people to watch the injustice as it was being perpetrated. Is that fair? Jesus, aren't you on the side of justice? What's going on here? Don't you see what will happen tomorrow at 7 a.m.? Nobody will show up! Can you blame them?

Imagine yourself as a member of a school board. Would you pay a teacher who worked hard for nine months the same amount that you paid a substitute who worked only the last week of school? Of course not! That would be contrary to every good business principle of just behavior toward an employee. This story appears to fly in the face of justice and good moral behavior. Jesus, what in the world are you trying to teach us?

Imagine yourself dealing with your children this way. One child not only does his or her duties well, but even goes beyond good behavior and has an attitude of helpfulness. Would you give this child the same allowance as one who does little or nothing? God, what are you trying to teach your children in this story?

Imagine that you are a member of a church council in a congregation with two pastors, one who is the senior pastor and has 25 years experience as a leader, preacher, and administrator and the other who is still "wet behind the ears" and just out of seminary. Not only is the assistant pastor inexperienced, but he never shows up to work until 11 a.m. There are those on the council who think that this assistant pastor should be fired. Would you pay these two pastors the same amount of salary? Wouldn't the lazy pastor just get lazier? How could a church operate effectively like that?

We have a major problem if this parable is about labor relations. *Of course, that is not the theme of the story.* This is not a moral example story about how to pay employees. The clue that unravels the mystery of the parable of the laborers is that *this is a story about God and the kingdom of God.* This is a story about how God works in relationship to his kingdom. In the kingdom of God, the just rewards theory of business doesn't work.

This Story Is About The Kingdom Of God And The Problem Of Murmuring

None of the parables of Jesus is a moral example story. If we understand the parables that way, we will be misled. Every parable of Jesus is intended to puncture religious preconceptions. That is particularly true of the parable of the laborers and their different times of arrival for work. In this story there are two preconceptions that are punctured. The first is about just rewards in the kingdom of God. The second is about envy and murmuring.

The preconception that in his kingdom God will work the way we work by rewarding people for good works is punctured by the disproportionate pay at the end of the story. The tendency toward complaining about how God works is exposed by the reversal of the first and the last. It is possible that we will come to an "aha moment" as we read or hear this story if we are willing to have our preconceptions and our negative attitudes examined.

How do we get to the "aha moment" in this story? How do we peel back a layer of apparent meaning and get at what Jesus is really talking about? Maybe two stories, two key concepts, and two songs will help.

Two Stories

The first story is in the front-side context of the parable. In Matthew 19:27-30, Peter has just asked a question about just rewards for having left everything and following Jesus. "What will we have at the end?" he asks. "What will the rewards be for our sacrifices?"

The "aha moment" begins to break through as Jesus explains to Peter that there is more than enough to go around at the end for those who serve him well, but that seeking rewards is not the way of selfless service. Jesus says the same thing at the end of this story of Peter that he says at the end of the parable. "Many who are first will be last, and the last will be first."

Pop! There goes one preconception. God does not work in heaven as we work on earth. Motivation is important to God and he doesn't like the motivation of those who are trying to get personal rewards for what they do for him.

The second story that may be of help comes from Eugene Lowery. As a child in Wichita, Kansas, Lowery had a feeling of being cheated when he first encountered the parable of the laborers. A group of long-time members of his Methodist church were talking about this parable. Someone said, "You know, it's just not fair. You mean to tell me that we who have been faithful to the church, given our money and time, always lived the straight and narrow — you mean to tell me that when we get to heaven, we'll be joined there by that guy who's always done whatever he wanted, and really lived it up, until his deathbed conversion experience? You mean the same heaven? Just isn't fair."[11]

To Lowery as a child, that argument seemed to hold a lot of truth, but what was missing from that conversation was the radical concept of grace that Jesus uses here and elsewhere. The word "radical" does not mean way out in right field. "Radical" doesn't mean extremely liberal or conservative. The original meaning of the word "radical" is "going to the root of something." The root of salvation is grace, God's saving action toward us in Christ, our only hope of salvation. We don't go to heaven as a reward for our good works. We do good works because we discover the amazing grace of God. In terms of our parable, this concept of grace is driven home by the question: "Don't I have the right to do what I want with my own money?" (Matthew 20:15a).

Two Concepts

The first concept has to do with the vertical relationship of Christianity. The second has to do with the horizontal dimension. The vertical and the horizontal dimensions form a cross, the ultimate symbol of the Christian faith.

The first concept that helps us understand this parable is grace. "We are saved by grace through faith," Saint Paul writes in

Ephesians 2:8-9. There is no other way to get to heaven except the way that God has provided. Good works are necessary for a Christian, not to get to heaven, but as an expression of gratefulness to God for all that he has done.

The second concept has to do with the motivation for doing good works for our neighbors. In the time of the Reformation, Martin Luther radically horizontalized good works. That means that he showed that the Bible points us to do good works for our neighbor, not as a way for us to get to heaven, but as a way of selfless service out of gratitude for all that God has done for us. The realization of the proper motivation for good works can be an "Aha moment" in our understanding the parable of the laborers. Grace means that God is generous and that we are called to be generous in good works to our neighbors. Generosity out of gratefulness is the opposite of envy and complaining.

Envy and complaining indicate that we do not understand the heavenly Father's grace and generosity. "Are you envious because I am generous?" the owner in the parable asks the murmuring laborers (Matthew 20:15b). It is only God's generosity that makes it possible for us to enter the kingdom of heaven. Murmuring about God's generosity is clear evidence that we do not understand the nature of our Father. Envy and complaining emerge as we focus on comparing our pay or benefits with fellow workers. If you compare yourself to God, you will discover that you come up on the short end and that the only proper response is gratefulness for what you receive.

Two Songs That Might Help

In addition to two stories about God's kingdom and two concepts about God's way to see things, it may be of some help to consider two songs, one religious, the other secular. The first song is a reminder that God is with us from birth till death.

John Ylvisaker wrote "Borning Cry" to help us see that God's grace permeates our lives, from beginning to end.

> *I was there to hear your borning cry. I'll be there when you are old. I rejoiced the day you were baptized to see your life unfold.*[12]

111

Since we have a God like that, who watches after us when we are born, when we are teenagers, when we marry and go through troubles, and who will be there with us when we die, we do good works out of gratefulness, not to seek reward. Did I hear an "aha" from someone?

The second song is a Broadway show tune about music, rhythm, and love. It is a secular song, but when the last line is connected to this parable, the secular suddenly becomes religious. The last line may cause someone to say, "Aha, now I understand God's word."

> *I got rhythm.*
> *I got music*
> *I got my man.*
> *Who could ask for anything more?*

Our God is in the marketplace looking and searching for anyone who will come and work for him. Our God is generous beyond belief, giving us grace far beyond what we deserve, miles beyond what we have earned. Our God wants us to come at 7:00 a.m. and enjoy as much of the work as we can, but if we come later, even just before quitting time, he is glad to have us in his kingdom. Aha.

This is a story about grace that will not be silenced. It is a story that can raise us from our sins. It is a story stronger than death. Aha.

Who could ask for anything more? Aha.

Points To Ponder

1. *Matthew 19:27-30* is about Peter who in his outbursts reveals our human nature. Examine Peter's self-centered statement and question in the light of the gospel. "We have left everything to follow you! What then will there be for us?" A paraphrase of the question may be helpful. "What reward will come to us for all the sacrifices we make and the good deeds we do?"

112

2. *William Barclay, the Bible commentator*, says that there are three great laws of the Christian life that emerge from the story of Peter's desire for reward.

   a. It is always true that he who shares Christ's campaign will share in Christ's victory.

   b. It is always true that the Christian will receive far more than ever he has to give up, but what he receives is not new material possessions but a new fellowship, human and divine.

   c. Finally, Jesus lays it down that there will be surprises in the final assessment ... Those who were humble on earth will be great in heaven and those who were great in this world will be humbled in the world to come.[13]

3. *The hours of 6 a.m. to 6 p.m. were the normal work day for a Jew in Jesus' day.* The eleventh hour of work was 5 p.m.

4. *This parable is both a warning and an invitation.* The warning is: "When you think about the kingdom of God, don't get caught in the world's system of rewards. The invitation is: "Come unto me and be comforted by the grace of God. All sinners who come by repentance and faith, no matter when they come in life, will be welcomed with open arms."

5. *The spirit* we have in coming is more important than the stage in life at which we come. The spirit of saying, "Live it up in life because you can always repent the last minute and be saved," is a spirit contrary to our Lord's spirit. On the other hand, if you only discover the error of your ways in the last hours of your life and truly repent, you will be accepted. In the case of the thief on the cross who truly repented, Jesus said, "Today you will be with me in Paradise."

6. *A Christian does not work for God in order to be paid a reward.* A Christian works for God out of gratitude for what God has done for him or her.

7. *The kingdom of heaven* has a place for everyone who comes out of true repentance and faith. It is never too late for a person to realize how much he or she has hurt God by disobedience and sin. It is never too late for that kind of repentance, turning away from self, and seeing God's hurt because of what we have done. That kind of repentance is quite different than a last minute turn to God out of fear of punishment and desire to get rewarded.

Questions For Personal Consideration
And/Or Group Discussion

1. If you are in a group study of this parable, talk about the thief on the cross who turned to Jesus and heard the words, "Today you shall be with me in Paradise."

2. If you are in a group, divide into two smaller groups. Group number one represents the world's ways of rewards for good works. Group number two represents the kingdom of God and God's grace. Have the two groups discuss the differences between the two kingdoms.

3. What does the statement that we are *in* the world, but not *of* the world mean?

4. What is the difference between success in this world and success in God's kingdom?

See **Digging Deeper**, p. 168 for further insights and applications.

Chapter Thirteen

A Puzzling Parable
With A Sharp Point

Luke 16:1-15

When I was a little boy, my mother often said something to me that I will never forget. When there was some kind of food on the table that I did not like, like spinach, I would say, "I don't want to eat it. I hate it." My mother would respond, "Ron, you don't hate it. You are just not very fond of it." She taught our three daughters to use these same words. In turn, they taught our eight grandchildren not to say, "I hate it," but instead to say, "I'm not very fond of it."

My mother also taught us that if we really liked some food to say, "I am really fond of it." I was "really fond" of cookies, candy, and cake. My mother had wise words of advice about these favorite foods. "Too many cookies, or too much candy and cake can be bad for you. You can be very fond of the wrong things."

The Puzzling Parable

Something like that is going on underneath the story of the shrewd manager. The topic is not food, but money. The Pharisees in our story are very fond of money. This story is a puzzling mystery in many respects. One of the first clues to unraveling the mystery of the dishonest money manager is found in my mother's words, "You can be very fond of the wrong things."

Another clue to unraveling this mysterious parable is to look at a key verse. Luke 16:14 is a verse that should get our attention. The *New International Version* translates Luke 16:14, "They [the

Pharisees] loved money." The *King James Version* translates this verse, "They were covetous." The *Revised Standard Version* says, "They were lovers of money." The translation (really a paraphrase) I like best is Phillips': "Now the Pharisees, who were very fond of money, heard all this with a sneer." The sneer comes from hearing a parable directed at them, a parable they did not like because they had distorted values about money.

The sneer of the Pharisees is a clue to getting at the heart of this parable. The sneer comes because the Pharisees try to justify themselves before the eyes of men, forgetting that God knows what is in the heart (Luke 16:15). Jesus' parable is about money. The Pharisees loved money too much. They were very fond of the wrong thing. Mammon was their God. By focusing on money, they had missed the real focus of life which is God. "No servant can serve two masters. Either he will hate the one and love the other, or he will be devoted to the one and despise the other. You cannot serve God and money" (Luke 16:13).

This last statement is the one that gave rise to the sneer. In trying to interpret a puzzling parable, sometimes we should look for a clue at the end of the story. Here at the end, Jesus shows that money can be a distracting attraction in life causing us to miss the meaning of life. The meaning of life is to be found in our relationship with God. It is not money that is the problem, but an inordinate focus on money that can be our undoing. "What is highly valued among men is detestable in God's sight" (Luke 16:15b). Elsewhere the Bible puts it this way: "The love of money is the root of all evil" (1 Timothy 6:10). Not money, but being overly fond of money, is the root of the problem of the Pharisees in our story and the root of the problem many people have today.

What we have here is a reversal of values. What is highly valued among people is possessions, land, honor, and money. What is highly valued in the kingdom of God? A relationship with God and relationships with people that include gracious acts toward people, faith in people, love for people, and forgiveness of people — these are the things which Jesus says have real value. Money is not meant to give us superiority over people, but for use to help people. Using one's possessions for people is called good stewardship. Understanding the biblical concept of stewardship is a big clue in solving the mystery of this puzzling parable.

When I think about stewardship, I always think of the heroes and heroines of the faith who set good examples by the way they use money and possessions to meet the needs of people. Saint Francis of Assisi and Mother Teresa of Calcutta come to mind. So does a little lady in Lebanon, Indiana, who will be permanently fixed in the balcony of my mind as someone who understood and practiced the biblical principles of stewardship.

Ada Gleb is one of my balcony people. Although Ada has been dead for a number of years, she is up there in the balcony of my mind. I can still see her and hear her. I can vividly remember some of her actions to help people. Although she never finished high school, Ada was a great professor of practical theology in the first church I served in Lebanon, Indiana, starting in 1960.

Ada Gleb taught me more about stewardship than all the professors at my seminary combined. She was a widow, a poor widow who lived in a run down house on the south side of town. Her clothes were clean, but not fancy. She drove an old car. She never talked much about stewardship, but her actions spoke louder than words. She put faith into action by using money for God's work and other people.

When I came out of seminary, I was called to be the pastor of a very small congregation in Lebanon, Indiana. The small congregation worshiped in a garage. Most of the members were not rich by the standards of the world. Ada was one of the poorest of the poor, but she was one of the top givers in the congregation. When I asked her about it, she humbly said that as a little girl she had learned to tithe, to give ten percent of her income to the church off the top before bills were paid. She did not have much income now, she said. It was mostly Social Security income, but she was glad to share it for the work of God.

At the time, I was making $6,200 a year. That small salary did not go far in trying to house, feed, and clothe our growing family of four. As a matter of fact, we could not afford to buy new clothes for our baby, our three-year-old, and ourselves. We were dependent on our parents giving our family clothes for Christmas, Easter,

Valentine's Day, and other holidays. When my wife had a miscarriage, we could not afford to pay the hospital bill.

When it came time to pledge for the work of the church, I looked at what Ada Gleb was giving and said, "I guess if she can tithe on her meager resources, I can too." The seminary had taught me nothing about personal stewardship. That is why I turned to "Professor Ada Gleb."

When the church grew and we had a building fund drive, Ada gave a large pledge above her tithe. "How can you do that?" I asked. "No problem," she said in a matter fact way, "I will just take the money out of my savings account each month." Ada knew that we needed the new church building. Her attitude of gracious giving inspired me to raise my giving level from ten percent to eighteen percent in order to build the new church building.

When Ada died, she left me $1,000 out of her small estate. That inheritance money was so precious that my wife and I could not spend it for any possessions. In Ada's name, we gave the money to a college student who had been thrown out of her house and was struggling to pay tuition to go to college. That college student went on to get a doctor's degree.

"Professor Ada" was fond of the right things. She was fond of God and his church. She was fond of people who needed the gospel and who had physical needs. She helped people with money. That too is a clue to unravel the mystery of the parable of the shrewd manager.

Jesus said, "I tell you, use worldly wealth to gain friends for yourselves, so that when it is gone, you will be welcomed into eternal dwellings" (Luke 16:9). I will be glad to testify for Ada should I be called upon as a witness on the Judgment Day. So will the college student who was able to get started at college because of Ada's $1,000.

It is possible to be "really fond" of the right things in life. It is also possible to be "really fond" of the wrong things. That brings us to another clue in the mystery of the parable with a puzzling point. In looking for clues about the meaning of parables, we should always ask, "What is Jesus trying to do here?"

The Nature Of Parables

In many of his parables, Jesus is trying to upset the equilibrium of his hearers. That is certainly true with this parable. Jesus is trying to work a reversal, upsetting his hearers with a big kingdom surprise. He is trying to pop preconceptions that will only get his hearers into trouble. He is doing it on purpose. He wants to help his hearers think about their value systems. No wonder the Pharisees sneered. People have trouble making changes in their lives, especially big changes. One man put it this way, "I don't have any trouble making changes in my life as long as I do not have to act differently." Ugh.

The nature of Jesus' parables is to serve as a wake up call to people who are missing the purpose of life. Many of the parables of Jesus are like a bucket of cold water thrown in our faces to wake us up to what life is really about.

The parables of Jesus are not moral example stories. If this parable were a moral example story, we would be in real trouble. The hero of this parable is an unjust rascal who is trying to save his own neck by working a compromise settlement with his master's debtors. Where is the integrity in his actions? Where is the moral example for our young people here? Why should we hold up a man who is "cooking the books" and then wiggles out of his troubles by compromised settlements? What is Jesus driving at?

Jesus tells the story of the shrewd steward who "cooked the account books" not because the man is a moral example, but because he wants to tell us about real values in the kingdom of God compared to the false values of this world. In a parable, the thing to look for is the point of tension to which the parable is addressed. Here that point of tension is the Pharisees' view of money and possessions. We are stewards, not owners. If we think of ourselves as owners, our possessions will possess us. "You cannot serve God and mammon" Jesus says.

In addition to the point of tension in the story told 2,000 years ago, parables address the points of tension in our lives today. The parables of Jesus are stories to remember. If we let them do their job, they will come rushing out of the past and wake us up today. If we really listen to what Jesus is saying, we actualize the past telling and experience the power and presence of the Lord today. In order to understand this parable we need to stand under the storyteller and hear the words as if we are hearing them addressed to us. To hear a parable of Jesus in the right way, we must hear it from the inside, as participants.

Eugene Lowry, in his book, *How to Preach a Parable*, says that in order to understand a parable, we must look for the itch, before we can feel the scratch. We must sense the tension, before we can receive relief of the tension. We must place ourselves in the puzzling setting before we can see the resolution to the puzzle. Lowry calls this "finding the focus of the story."[14]

All this talk about participation and finding the focus notwithstanding, what do we do with the steward who is a rascal making shady deals with shady debtors and a master who commends the shrewdness of his steward for the deals he makes? In Luke 16:8-9 we read:

> *The master commended the dishonest manager because he acted shrewdly. For the people of this world are more shrewd in dealing with their own kind than are the people of light. I tell you, use worldly wealth to gain friends for yourselves, so that when it is gone, you will be welcomed into eternal dwellings.*

What Is The Sharp Point
In This Puzzling Parable?

The sharp point of this parable is that the master commends the use of money for people, instead of the use of money for pride, power, position, and possessions. In other words, the value of money and possessions comes to a dead end when we die. The sharp point of this parable is felt when we realize that money and the material goods it buys will do us no good when we arrive at eternity and face the judgment of God.

Helmut Thielicke, in his book of parables titled *The Waiting Father*, puts it this way:

It is made perfectly clear to us that one day every one of us will be left destitute. The day will come when we shall stand naked before God, unable to answer him once in a thousand times. We shall be stripped of all things in which we put our confidence here below. We shall stand before the throne of God without title, without money, without home, without reputation — in utter poverty.[15]

That is the sharp point of the powerful but puzzling parable in Luke 16. One day we will have to face God. We cannot fool God. He knows our motives and our actions. God knows our hearts (Luke 16:15). He also knows all about our checkbooks. He knows whether we have used our money to help people or for self-aggrandizement and power over people.

The Bible tells us two things about the judgment. First, and foremost, God is very fond of us. He desires to save us, not send us to hell. First Timothy 2:4 says, "God ... wants all ... to be saved." Jesus loves us so much that he would rather die on the cross than let us go. Second, the Bible tells us that God is not mocked. What a person sows, he shall also reap.

One day we shall all stand before the throne of God in utter poverty. In that place where money is neither received nor spent, and where all values have been turned upside down, God will ask, "Who will testify for you?" The final verdict on how we shall spend eternity comes from God who knows whether of not we believe in him and whether or not we have done what he wants us to do with money and possessions.

Earlier in this chapter I said that I would like to bring testimony for Ada Gleb at the time of her appearance before the throne of God. I will speak up for her and say, "She was a sinner who needed redemption. She found that redemption in Jesus. She is very fond of you, Lord."

"Yes, I know," I can imagine God saying.

"She was very fond of people, too. She was a great teacher of stewardship."

"Yes, I know."

What will happen then? I can only imagine it, but I think God may say something like this: "Ada, I have heard what has been said in your behalf. I have heard that others want you to be with them in the eternal habitations. Blessed are you, my faithful child. You have made unrighteous mammon righteous because you used it to feed the poor and hungry and clothe the needy. I am very fond of you. Enter into the joy of your master."

Money should not become an idol for us. Money is a servant. Believers are stewards of money and the gifts that come from God. Believers are grateful for what has been accomplished for them by the cross of Christ. That cross has secured a place for us in eternity. In the last analysis, that is the only thing that matters. Everything else passes away.

This parable is a warning and an invitation. In the words of my mother, the warning is: "You can get into big trouble if you are really fond of the wrong things." The invitation is to come unto the Lord whose arms are wide open to meet you and greet you on the shores of eternity with these words, "Enter into the joy of your Master."

Points To Ponder

1. *1 Timothy 6:17.* "The love of money is the root of all evil." Note that is not money, but the distorted and inordinate love of money that ruins people.

2. *A bad man's good example.* The steward in our story is a rascal. He is a slave who was left in charge of the estate of the absentee landlord. Guilty of embezzlement, he is hardly a hero. Yet, he did one thing right. He used money for people. Jesus is not urging us to be like this bad man, but to be wise in this one way. Using our money and possessions for people can make an eternal difference.

3. *Luke 16:8*. If Christians were as clever and eager to do good as evil men are to attain money or power, the world would be better off.

4. *Luke 16:9*. Material possessions should be used for God's work and to cement human relations.

5. *Luke 16:10-11*. A person's way of fulfilling a small task may be proof of his fitness for a bigger task.

6. *Luke 16:13*. No one can serve two masters. We either serve God as our master, or another master will come along and fill in the void. Serving God is a full time job. If you try to make it a part time job, another master will get a foothold in your life.

Questions For Personal Consideration And/Or Group Discussion

1. List several examples of how the love of money can be the root of evil (1 Timothy 6:17).

2. Do you agree or disagree with this statement: "Your wallet or your purse may have more to do with your salvation than your hymn book."

   Explain your answer.

3. Who are some of the balcony people in your life?

4. What did these balcony people teach you?

See **Digging Deeper**, p. 169, for further insights and applications.

Chapter Fourteen

The Man Who Never Noticed

Luke 16:19-31

Have you ever overlooked something really important and then looking back said, "How could I have missed that? It was so obvious. I should have seen it." That happened to me at a worship service at King of Glory Lutheran Church in Fountain Valley, California, recently. When it came time for the offering, I skipped right over it. I forgot it completely. I glanced at my bulletin and my service book and just did not notice the offering. As the people left the church, the ushers held out the offering plates, smiled and said, "The pastor neglected to take the offering." I felt like a fool, but at least the ushers saved the day. Sometimes we can recuperate from something we neglect. Sometimes we cannot recuperate.

In the parable of the rich man who did not notice, we have an example of neglect from which no recuperation is possible. Dives, which is Latin for rich, doesn't notice Lazarus, a beggar, outside his door. When he dies, Dives goes to hell. In life, his problem was that he did not notice God's ways and God's Word.

Taking Notice Of God's Ways

God has his ways; we have ours. These two ways are often distinctly different. "My ways are not your ways," says the Lord. If we do not notice the difference, and make the appropriate adjustments, we, like Dives, will face serious consequences.

There are at least three differences between God's ways and human ways that Dives did not notice. As we consider these three, perhaps we will pay more attention to God's ways and avoid the ultimate consequences of not noticing. In this parable, God pops at least three misconceptions that can send us to hell.

First, there is more to life than the here and now. There is a hereafter where we will spend eternity. Dives had a misconception that life consisted only of the gathering of wealth, eating, drinking, and being merry. Pop. There goes misconception number one.

God's ways include a strong emphasis on the life to come. Money and pleasure are not wrong in themselves. A rich man or woman can have a focus on serving God in the here and now and living with God in the hereafter. But riches and earthly pleasures have a way of distracting us from focusing our lives on God's ways. Heaven or hell are at the end of our journey. Dives did not notice what is at the end of life's journey.

One Sunday it was very hot in Dallas, Texas. The air conditioner at Christ Lutheran Church was broken. On the spot, the pastor decided to preach a short ten word sermon. He got into the pulpit and said, "Hot, isn't it? Hell's like that. Don't go there. Amen."

That is a good summary of what Jesus has in mind in telling the parable of the man who did not notice. The way to avoid going to hell is to pay attention to God's ways instead of human ways. God's ways focus on living in this world, but not being of this world. Human ways focus on gathering treasures on earth.

Jesus said, "Do not store up for yourselves treasures on earth, where moth and rust destroy, and where thieves break in and steal. But store up for yourselves treasures in heaven, where moth and rust do not destroy, and where thieves do not break in and steal. For where your treasure is, there your heart will be also" (Matthew 6:19-21).

Paying inordinate attention to the abundance of things, Dives did not pay attention to the hereafter. He wound up in hell.

Second, you can go to hell for not noticing the needy. Dives did not notice Lazarus right outside his door. He missed an opportunity to meet human need because he was self-absorbed. Many people today have the same problem.

In Matthew 25:31-46, Jesus talks about the ultimate separation that will take place in afterlife based on whether or not we have noticed the poor, the prisoners, the hungry, and thirsty.

When the Son of Man comes in his glory, and all the angels with him, he will sit on his throne in heavenly glory. All the nations will be gathered before him and he will separate the people one from another as a shepherd separates the sheep from the goats. He will put the sheep on his right and the goats on his left.

Then the King will say to those on his right, "Come, you who are blessed by my Father; take your inheritance, the kingdom prepared for you since the creation of the world. For I was hungry and you gave me something to eat, I was thirsty and you gave me something to drink, I was a stranger and you invited me in, I needed clothes and you clothed me, I was sick and you looked after me, I was in prison and you came to visit me."

Then the righteous will answer him, "Lord, when did we see you hungry and feed you, or thirsty and give you something to drink? When did we see you a stranger and invite you in, or needing clothes and clothe you? When did we see you sick or in prison and go to visit you?"

The King will reply, "I tell you the truth, whatever you did for one of the least of these brothers of mine, you did for me."

Wow! That is what it will be like to wake up in heaven someday and discover that in noticing the needy and ministering to them, we were actually ministering to the Lord himself. Notice that the righteous are so focused on the needs of the others that no thought is given to heavenly reward for good deeds. The righteous are genuinely surprised to find that in noticing the needy, their good deeds were noticed by the Almighty. We pick up the story in verse 41.

Then he (the King) will say to those on his left, "Depart from me, you who are cursed , into the eternal fire prepared for the devil and his angels. For I was hungry and you gave me nothing to eat, I was thirsty and you gave me nothing to drink, I was a stranger and you did not invite me in, I needed clothes and you did not clothe me."

127

> *They also will answer, "Lord, when did we see you*
> *hungry or thirsty or a stranger or needing clothes or*
> *sick or in prison, and did not help you?"*
> *He will reply, "I tell you the truth, whatever you*
> *did not do for one of the least of these, you did not do*
> *for me."*

Then they will go away to eternal punishment, but the righteous to eternal life.

Pop! There goes another misconception. What you neglect to do for the needy is neglecting God who dwells in the needy. That is why Lazarus is so important. He is one in whom God dwells. Dives not only neglected Lazarus. By neglecting Lazarus, he also neglected God.

Third, you can go to hell for neglecting God's way of salvation. That way of salvation is faith active in love. Good deeds do not get you into heaven. That is clear in Matthew 25:31-46 where we learn that the righteous are surprised that their good deeds were noticed. The righteous do good deeds because they discovered God's goodness by faith. Faith alone saves, but genuine faith expresses itself in good deeds. Genuine faith means noticing that God notices the needy and therefore we should notice them too.

The Pharisees did not understand true faith. They tried to justify themselves on the basis of good works. They looked down on the needy and trusted their own way of salvation. The parable of the shrewd manager (Luke 16:1-13), about using money for people, was addressed to the Pharisees. Luke 16:14-15 says, "The Pharisees, who loved money, heard all this and were sneering at Jesus. He said to them, 'You are the ones who justify yourselves in the eyes of men, but God knows your hearts. What is highly valued among men is detestable in God's sight.' " Then came the knockout blow.

Jesus told the Pharisees the second parable about the man who never noticed. They still were not paying attention to God's way of salvation. They expected Jesus to praise them for their good deeds of following rules and regulations. Instead, Jesus points to good deeds for people that come from real faith. The Pharisees were following their own ways of salvation by works of the law. Pop. There goes another misconception.

The Bible teaches that God wants all people to be saved. Stubborn resistance to God's way of salvation is what sends people to hell. People send themselves to hell by not paying attention to God's ways. Stubborn resistance can send us to hell.

Johnny was a stubborn man. He came to a bank and said to Robert, the banker, "Please cash my check."

Robert replied, "Okay, Johnny, but you will have to turn the check over and endorse it."

"I won't endorse it. I just want you to cash it," Johnny said.

"If you don't endorse it, I cannot cash it," Robert replied.

"Then I will take the check to the other bank and talk to James. He will cash it for me," Johnny said as he stomped out of the bank.

"What can I do for you today?" James asked.

"Please cash my check," Johnny said.

"Sure," James replied, "just turn it over and endorse it."

"I'm not going to endorse it. I just want you to cash it," Johnny said defiantly.

James reached through the bars of the bank window, grabbed Johnny by the lapels and crashed his head on the marble counter top several times. "Now sign the check," James said.

Johnny did what he was told. When he returned to see his friend Robert, Johnny said, "James cashed my check."

"He made you endorse it first, didn't he?" Robert asked.

"Yes, but he explained it first," Johnny said.

This parable is an attempt to explain the ways of God in no uncertain terms to stubborn people who try to follow their own ways instead of God's ways. Sometimes it takes some head banging to get our attention to God's ways. Sometimes it also takes some head banging to get our attention to God's Word.

Taking Notice Of God's Word

In the first part of the parable of the man who never noticed Lazarus, the beggar, Lazarus finds himself in heaven, called Abraham's side (or Abraham's bosom in another translation). On the other hand, Dives, the rich man, finds himself in hell because he stubbornly clung to his ways instead of God's ways. Dives did not follow God's ways because he did not take notice of God's Word. We know that because of the second part of the parable. We pick up the story in verse 27.

After being told that there was a great gulf between heaven and hell, Dives asks that Lazarus be sent back to his father's house to reveal God's ways to his five brothers. "Let him warn them, so that they will not also come to this place of torment," he says (Luke 16:28). In other words, Dives recognizes that his brothers need a knock on the head to wake up to the true values of life.

"Abraham replied, 'They have Moses and the Prophets; let them listen to them' " (Luke 16:29). In other words, the Word of God is a big enough bang on the head to shake the foundations of anyone. Let me paraphrase this verse: "Let people read and follow the Bible. It is clear enough for anyone."

Dives is not satisfied. He continues to argue, "No, Father Abraham ... if someone from the dead goes to them, they will repent" (Luke 16:30). "A spectacular miracle will do it," Dives thinks. "A spectacular miracle would have awakened me. It will also awaken my brothers." Many people think that they would believe if only God would send some spectacular miracle. Contrary to that kind of thinking, Jesus resisted the lure of the spectacular as a way to wake people up. If you go back to the temptations of Christ in the wilderness, you will discover that one of these temptations is that Jesus should throw himself down from the tower of the Temple and be saved by the angels of God. Jesus says, "No," to the lure of the spectacular. In this parable he says, "No," to the request of Dives to send Lazarus back from the dead.

"If they do not listen to Moses and the Prophets, they will not be convinced even if someone rises from the dead" (Luke 16:31). In other words, the ways of God are pointed out clearly in the Word of God. If you do not pay attention to the Word of God, you will not truly repent and believe, even if you see a spectacular miracle. Pop! There goes another misconception about God and people.

We think that if God would just set up a megaphone on cloud seventeen and announce that he had sent his Son into the world to redeem people from their sins that those who stubbornly resist this way of salvation would wake up and believe. God knows that this way of the spectacular might appear to get people turned around, but that in truth, this would not be a lasting turn back to God. What causes repentance, a turn to God that lasts, is if people will believe what God has revealed in his Word.

That is why what makes a difference in life is teaching and preaching that is solidly fixed on the Word of God. That Word of God comes to us in three ways.

First and foremost, Jesus himself is the Word of God. The church's one foundation is Jesus Christ, her Lord. Teaching and preaching Christ as the way of salvation means that a church is built on the solid foundation of Jesus Christ.

Second, the Bible is God's Word. We speak of the Bible as God's Word because the Bible, here called "Moses and the Prophets," helps us see the ways of God clearly. People who are devoted to studying and learning from the Bible notice that applying the Word of God means paying close attention to the needs of our neighbors.

Third, preaching of Christ from the Bible is God's Word. Preaching, as the early church viewed it, is more than what the pastor says on Sunday morning from the pulpit. Preaching is what all Christians do as they witness to Christ as the way of salvation. Preaching means saying the right thing, in the right way, at the right time under the guidance of the Holy Spirit so that people are turned to God as their hope of salvation.

Dives and his five brothers missed God's ways because they did not pay attention to the Word of God. We are invited to pay attention to God's Word so that we do not make the same mistake.

As I said at the beginning of this chapter, I made a mistake one Sunday by neglecting to take up the offering. A more serious mistake is made by people who do not take notice of the offering of salvation God makes through Jesus Christ.

Points To Ponder

1. *Names can be revealing.* In this parable, the villain is often called Dives, which is Latin for "rich." The danger of riches is that they can sometimes keep us from noticing what is really important in life. The name Lazarus means "God is my help." The Bible teaches that God is our help and salvation.

2. *Lazarus, the beggar, waited for crumbs from Dives' table.* There were no forks or knives or napkins in Jesus' day. Food was eaten with the fingers. Hands were wiped on the bread that was served. In wealthy homes, the bread was thrown out after the meal was served. This bread was the crumbs that Lazarus would have gladly eaten.

3. *The lack of compassion for the needy* got Dives into serious trouble after he died. This lack of compassion meant that Dives was in serious trouble before he died. He just did not notice the trouble in which he found himself. Like the Pharisees in Luke 16:14-15, he majored in minors like luxury, exotic and costly food, and pride of possessions.

4. *Luke 16:22 refers to Abraham's side.* Abraham was the first patriarch of the faith. This reference is to heaven. God's spokesperson from eternity is Abraham.

5. *Dives' desire to have a warning sent to his brothers* is denied because Moses and the Prophets point to the ways of God. The brothers and all of us should pay attention to the teachings of the Law that shows us our need for a Savior and the Prophets who predict the coming of Christ.

6. Moses, symbolizing the Law, and Elijah, symbolizing the Prophets, both acknowledged Jesus as Lord at the transfiguration (Mark 9:2-4 and Matthew 17:1-3).

Questions For Personal Consideration
And/Or Group Discussion

1. Does this parable teach that all rich people go to hell? If not, why did this rich man go to hell?

2. Does this parable teach that all poor people go to heaven? If not, what does it take for a person to go to heaven?

3. What is the problem with the five brothers of Dives?

4. What are the difficulties of helping the needy today?

See **Digging Deeper**, p. 170, for further insights and applications.

Chapter Fifteen

The Pushy Widow

Luke 18:1-8

This is a Jewish story. That is important for at least two reasons. First, Jewish women tend to be the boss of the house. Ask any Jewish boy: "Did your mother run the home?" The answer is likely to be, "Yes!"

The traditional Jewish religion of Jesus' day favored men over women. Men sat in prominent places in the synagogue. Women sat in the back of the synagogue or in the balcony. Jewish men could get a divorce easily by going down to the town well, walk around it saying, "I divorce you ... I divorce you ... I divorce you," and it would be an accomplished fact. Jewish women of Jesus' day could not get a divorce, even if their husbands were cruel. Only the men were allowed to be rabbis. Women were not even supposed to discuss theology.

All that notwithstanding, God has a sense of humor. The Jewish women not only ruled the home with an iron fist; it was only through the lineage of your mother, not your father, that you could be a real Jew. Even to this day, if you have a Jewish father, but not a Jewish mother, you are not really Jewish. I know. The name Lavin is Jewish, but I am not really Jewish. My father was Jewish; my mother was Irish Catholic. That, by the way, is not exactly a pure Scandinavian heritage for a Lutheran pastor!

Strong Jewish women are part of the heritage behind this story.

The second reason that we need to note that this is a Jewish story is that in Jewish stories, the protagonist need not be good. In the parable of the shrewd manager (Luke 16:1-15), the protagonist is a manager who cuts a deal with the master's debtors. That is anything but an moral example of how we should act. Jesus was a Jew. His parables frequently lift up people who, representing God, are strange heroes. That is true of the parable of the pushy widow. The figure for God is an uncaring and corrupt judge. In parables like this, we need to hear the unspoken words, "How much more God...."

God is not like the uncaring and corrupt judge who responded to the pushy widow. If the evil and self-centered judge responded positively to the persistence of the widow who would not take "No" for an answer, how much more will God respond to his own people?

Consider two parallel parables in Luke 11:5-13. In the first one, Jesus sets a friend, who needs bread for a visitor and bangs on the door of a neighbor at midnight to get some, as an example of how to pray. The bold host is an example of how we should come banging at God's door in prayer. "Knock and the door will be opened to you," Jesus says (Luke 11:9). If the neighbor will give the bread to the bold host, *how much more* will God answer prayers when people persist? That question is never stated. It is implied in the first of the parallel parables in Luke 11. In the second parallel parable the "how much more" is stated in no uncertain terms.

Luke 11:11-13 is the parable of the father who would never give a snake to a son asking for a fish or a scorpion to a son asking for an egg. Jesus ends this story by saying: "If you then, though you are evil, know how to give good gifts to your children, *how much more will your Father in heaven give the Holy Spirit to those who ask him!*" (Luke 11:13).

With these introductory remarks, let us hasten on to five possible explanations to one of the questions raised by this parable. Why does God delay in answering prayer?

Five Possible Reasons Why God
Delays In Answering Prayer

We know why the corrupt judge in the parable delays in answering the honest request of the widow, but why does God delay in answering prayer? The honest answer is that we do not know why God delays in answering prayer. We will not know until we arrive at heaven's gates and can ask God himself why the answers to prayer sometimes seem so slow in coming. Here on earth, we can only make intelligent guesses at why good, sincere prayers seem to go unanswered for long periods of time.

Before we look at these five possibilities for God's delay in answering prayers, we should look at the nature of the judge in our parable. William Barclay, the New Testament scholar, describes the judge in Jesus' parable in a helpful way.

> *The judge was clearly not a Jewish judge. All ordinary Jewish disputes were taken before the elders, and not into the public courts at all. If, under Jewish law, a matter was taken to arbitration, one man could not constitute a court. There were always three judges, one chosen by the plaintiff, one by the defendant, and one independently appointed.*
>
> *The judge was one of the paid magistrates appointed either by Herod or by the Romans. Such judges were notorious. Unless a plaintiff had influence and money to bribe his way to a verdict, he had no hope of ever getting his case settled. These judges were said to pervert justice for a dish of meat. People ... called them robber judges.*[16]

That explanation helps us determine why the widow had to be so pushy. Remember, as we look at God being represented in this parable by a robber judge, we must add, "how much more" God answers the prayers of his people. Yet our experience with prayer is that often God does not answer prayers quickly. Consider five possible reasons.

First, God delays in answering prayer to intensify our desires. Many people desire cheap, quick, easy answers to their prayers. Their desires are not heart-felt, passionate pleas, but superficial requests to God who is like the supernatural being in the story of Aladdin's lamp. In that story, the supernatural being exists to answer our wishes. That illusionary view of God is corrected time and again in the Bible.

Second, God delays in answering prayer to purify our motives. Our motives are not always high-minded. Sometimes by waiting we can go from "I want," "I demand," "I insist" prayers to seeking what is really best in God's eyes. Our motives can be purified by the period of not getting quick, easy answers.

Third, God delays in answering prayer to develop our patience. An immature woman once prayed, "I want more patience and I want it right now." One of the virtues of the Christian life is patience. That is a hard lesson to learn. Impatience means thinking that we are in charge in life and that others, including God, should do what we want, when we what, how we want it.

A nine-year-old boy went to a movie and heard the European male star demand from the beautiful screen heroine, "I vant, vhat I vant, vhen I vant it." He went home from the movie and decided to try the formula on his nine-year-old girlfriend. "I vant, vhat I vant, vhen I vant it," he said. She responded, "You'll get what I got, when I get it."

Patience is one of the things we can learn when we do not get immediate answers to our prayers. Waiting can teach us patience.

Fourth, God delays in answering prayers to encourage our persistence. God wants persistent witnesses for the faith. Christians meet resistance from unbelievers. They also meet indifference. If they gave up, many would not find saving faith. Persistent witness comes from learning to wait for God in prayer.

The early Christians were persecuted. The context of Luke 18:6-8 is the prediction of persecution for Christians. Justice will come, God promises, but you must be persistent in the face of the enemies of the faith. "And will not God bring about justice for his chosen one, who cry out to him day and night? Will he keep putting them off? I tell you, he will see that they get justice, and quickly" (Luke 18:7-8a).

Fifth, God delays in answering prayers because waiting is the true nature of faith. The last line of the parable seems to point us toward this explanation: "However, when the Son of Man comes, will he find faith on the earth?" (Luke 18:8b).

True faith means waiting because only by waiting do we understand that God's timetable and our timetable are not always the same. God sees the big picture. We only see small and often distorted portions of what is happening. Time is a major biblical category. The word that is often used to describe God's timing is *kairos*. *Kairos* means God's time, the fullness of time, the ripe, ready time. We live in what the Bible calls the *chronos*, from which we get our word chronology. Sometimes the *chronos* and the *kairos* are two very different ways to look at events and experiences. A third biblical word for time is *telos*, the end time, where, looking back, we will see the ways in which the *chronos* and the *kairos* have intersected in our lives.

True faith means waiting because God alone lives in the *telos*. He alone knows what is good for us. Sometimes what we think is good for us is the opposite of what we need. Sometimes what we think is bad for us is the very stuff out of which we draw nearer to God. For example, suffering is not a desirable state for us or loved ones, but many Christians testify that it was only in a time of suffering that they really turned their lives over to Christ as Lord and Savior.

Psalm 130:5-6 (RSV) elevates waiting to the state of faith where we learn to depend on and place our hopes on God's word.

> *I wait for the LORD, my soul waits,*
> *and in his word I hope;*
> *my soul waits for the LORD*
> *more than watchmen for the morning,*
> *more than watchmen for the morning.*

As noted earlier, we do not know all the reasons why God delays is answering prayers. We do know from this parable as well as other Bible passages that God loves persistence in his people who trust him enough to wait.

God Loves Persistence In His People

Jesus holds up this pushy widow in front of us as a pattern for prayer because God loves persistence in his people. Pushy people often irritate us. We don't like it if our wives or husbands get too pushy. We don't like it if our fathers or mothers get too pushy. We don't like pushy bosses or pushy sales people. Pushy means aggressive behavior. It is often objectionable, but in some cases is necessary.

In the case of the robber judge, "who neither feared God nor cared about men" (Luke 18:2), the aggressive behavior of the pushy widow was not only appropriate; it was essential. In this case, the pushy widow was assertive enough to get the justice she wanted and needed. While we may be technically correct to call this behavior persistent, that term may be too mild to describe accurately the passion of the woman who teaches us how to pray. Since "aggressive" is generally a negative term, we might use the term "assertive" to describe this widow. But, from my way of thinking, the best way to describe the pushy woman with a cause is to call her indomitable.

A stubborn Irish policeman named Shane McClellan and his wife Peggine were arguing about church, prayer, and the practice of faith. Shane refused to go to church. He was just too busy. "Shane McClellan, you are stubborn to the core," Peggine said.

"You are stubborn too," he replied.

"No," she said. "You are stubborn. I'm indomitable."

Peggine was a lot like the pushy widow in our parable. Peggine was unconquerable when it came to faith and prayer. Lucille Taylor was a lot like that too. When it came to faith prayer, Lucille was indomitable.

Lucille Taylor was the custodian in the 5,000 member St. Paul Lutheran Church I served in Davenport, Iowa, some years ago. I was her boss, but when it came to faith and prayer, she was often my teacher. She was a black Baptist who loved her church, loved her Lord, and often said so.

When our associate pastor, Bob Parker, had a heart attack and nearly died, we held a prayer service for his recovery in the sanctuary at St. Paul Lutheran Church. Bob Parker was given just one day to live.

Lucille was present for the prayer service. We Lutherans prayed heart-felt, but rather formal prayers for the recovery of our friend. When it was Lucille's turn, she prayed something like this:

God, this is Lucille. You know me and I know you. I want you to heal Bob Parker and do it pronto. We need him. He needs restored health so that he can continue to love people and show people faith. God, I know that you can heal him. I believe that you will do it. In Jesus' name. Amen.

My first reaction to Lucille's prayer was shock. "That is no way to talk to God," I thought. Then I remembered what Jesus said about prayer. "Ask and it will be given to you; seek and you will find; knock and the door will be opened to you. For everyone who asks receives; he who seeks finds; and to him who knocks, the door will be opened" (Luke 11:9-10).

After the prayer service, I asked Lucille what she thought about it. "It was very good," she said, "but you Lutherans are a little mild in your proper prayers."

Bob Parker, who had been given one day to live, lived another two years. I think that God delighted in all of the prayers of his people, but I believe that he especially liked the faith and prayer of the indomitable Lucille Taylor.

God loves that kind of faith and prayer. If you ask me how I know, I will point you toward the widow who sought justice from the uncaring and God-less judge in our parable. God does what he does on his own time schedule. His time is not always our time. God sometimes seems slow to answer our prayers, but that does not mean that he is not listening. Justice will be done. We are called to remain faithful, even when everything around us is falling apart. God will keep his word. But that brings us to the closing question of the parable of the pushy widow.

"However, when the Son of Man comes, will he find faith on the earth?" (Luke 18:8b).

Points To Ponder

1. *In the Bible, a widow often represents all who are needy.* This widow, like a lot of needy people, was on the short end of justice. Her indomitable spirit got her through to the unjust judge who neither cared about God nor man.

2. *Luke 18:1-5* contains Jesus' parable of the pushy widow. Luke 18:6-8 contains the application to those who are persecuted.

3. *Luke 11:5-13* should be studied side by side with Luke 18:1-8. Both passages are about the need for persistence in prayer by indomitable Christians.

4. *Luke 11:13* includes these important words, "... how much more will your Father in heaven give the Holy Spirit to those who ask him?"

5. *Jesus prayed in the Garden of Gethsemane* that "this cup" (the cross) pass from him. He prayed this prayer three times. Then he prayed, "Thy will be done." See Matthew 26:36-56; Mark 14:32-52; Luke 22:39-53; and John 18:1-12.

6. *The nature of mature prayer is waiting.* See Psalm 130:5-6. The mature Christian is called to pray with passion believing that God will answer prayer, but sometimes God's timing is different than our timing.

7. *Luke 18:4-5.* "Lest she ... wear me out" in the original Greek text literally reads, "Lest she come at last and beat me."[17] William Barclay says these verses could be translated, "Lest she give me a black eye."[18] The judge had a healthy respect for this widow's wrath.

8. *"When the Son of Man comes"* refers to the end of time. This is the time the Bible calls the *telos*. This is when the kingdom of God that we only know in part now will be revealed in fullness. That is when every knee shall bow and every tongue confess that Jesus is Lord to the glory of God. The ultimate question for this time is: "Will we be found faithful or not?"

Questions For Personal Consideration
And/Or Group Discussion

1. Do you agree or disagree with this statement: "We often desire cheap, quick, easy answers to our prayers." Explain your answer.

2. Compare prayer to Aladdin's lamp which brought instant magic answers to the one making the request that his wishes be answered.

3. What does the word "indomitable" mean?

See **Digging Deeper**, p. 171, for further insights and applications.

Chapter Sixteen

The Recovery
Of Guilt And Grace

Luke 18:9-14

Some years ago I was preparing a sermon titled "Disillusioned People." I was stuck. Writer's block moved in like a fog. I just could not find the right words for this sermon about people who were discouraged and disheartened. I stopped what I was doing and shared my predicament with my wife. She said, "Why don't you check the dictionary?"

When I went to the dictionary, I found that the word "disillusioned" means "freed from illusions." When I looked up the word "illusion," I found that it means "false ideas." Disillusioned means freed from illusions. While we generally use the word in a negative sense, "disillusioned" can be a very positive term. We all need to be freed from illusions.

In the parable of the Pharisee and the tax collector, both need to be freed from their illusions. The false idea that the self-righteous Pharisee has is that prayer is a matter of cataloging good deeds. The false idea that the tax collector has is that he is beyond help. The Pharisee thinks that he is justified before God because of the good works of the law that he has done. The tax collector thinks that since he is such a great sinner, nothing can justify him. Both are wrong. The Pharisee compares himself to other people and thinks that he is superior. The tax collector compares himself to God and thinks that he has no chance of redemption. Both are wrong.

Comparing Ourselves To Other People

To be justified before God means being made right with God. Justification means wholeness before God. We cannot be made right with God or made whole if we insist on comparing ourselves to others, finding their faults, and looking for a reward from God for our goodness. That is the dilemma of the Pharisee in the Temple in our story.

The Pharisee stood up and prayed about himself (or to himself): "God, I thank you that I am not like other men — robbers, evildoers, adulterers — or even like this tax collector" (Luke 18:11). He threw a sideward glance at the tax collector in the shadows standing at a distance away, beating his breast in repentance. That sideward glance is the problem.

When we look sideward, we can always find those who are worse than we are. Comparing ourselves to others, we will always find ways in which we are better than certain other people. The Pharisee went on to boast about what he did better than others: "I fast twice a week, and give a tenth of all I get" (Luke 18:12). In fact, he was better than robbers, evildoers, adulterers, and tax collectors; but to try to justify yourself on this kind of basis is to be filled with illusions about yourself.

A friend told me the story of the first time he heard this story as a child. His mother read it to him and then asked, "Now, who was the good man?" "The one who fasted, prayed, and gave lots of money to the church," the little boy said. "Let me read you the story again," the mother said. Afterward, she again asked, "Who is the one who is good in this story?" Again the boy answered, "The Pharisee. He did all of the right things." Once more, the mother read the parable to the child. Once more she asked, "Now think, son. Who is the good man in the parable?"

The little boy thought for a moment. Then he replied, "I still think that it is the Pharisee. I overheard you and Daddy complaining about paying taxes the other day. A tax collector must be an evil man." In fact, as we shall see, the tax collector in our story was evil, but that is not the point of the story. The point is that God made him good.

It is not easy to understand how an evil man can be good and a good man evil. Seeing ourselves as good is the illusion from which Jesus attempts to free us by telling this story. He is trying to disillusion us, taking us from illusions to the truth about justification. The key to understanding this parable is to look at justification. The story is not about doing right things or wrong things. This story is about justification before God.

In this parable about justification, Jesus gives us a peek into the hearts of two men in the Temple. Justification has to do with what is in the secret places in the heart. Justification has to do with the attitudes we have. The problem with the Pharisee in our story is that in the secret places of his heart, he was filled with pride. Pride is the wrong motivation for doing good deeds. Pride is the problem in the heart of the Pharisee.

T. S. Eliot, the poet, wrote: "The last temptation is the greatest treason, / To do the right thing for the wrong reason."

The Pharisee in our story was doing good things for the wrong reasons. He was doing works of the law to add to his list of good deeds for which he expected God to reward him. That kind of pride can get any of us in real trouble. That view of reward is precisely what gave rise to the Protestant Reformation.

Martin Luther saw people seeking to do good deeds with a view toward heavenly reward. He saw that the Roman Catholic Church of his day was teaching that you could go to heaven if you did the prescribed good deeds that the church promoted. He saw that the doctrine of spending less time in Purgatory by paying for indulgences was not only bad theology, but the exact opposite of what the Bible teaches about how one goes to heaven. Luther's insight was that we are justified before God only by grace through faith and not the works of the law (Ephesians 2:8-9). He read Saint Paul's words in Romans 1:17: "For in the gospel a righteousness from God is revealed, a righteousness that is by faith from first to last, just as it is written, 'The righteous will live by faith.' " Luther said, "Faith is the way of justification. Faith is the way of salvation. Faith alone is the way we go to heaven." The creed of the Reformation is: "Grace alone, faith alone, and Scripture alone."

Luther led the Reformation of the church of his day around the basic principle of this parable: Repentance for sin and faith in God is what makes us right with God. He rediscovered what Saint Paul had discovered before him.

Saint Paul, the former Pharisee, wrestled with the same illusion that the Pharisee in our parable had. He tried to justify himself before God by following the prescribed works of the law and comparing himself to other people. When he became a Christian, he discovered that his false idea about justification had not only gotten him into big trouble, but that many people of his day, even some people in the church, were being misled about the way of salvation. Paul wrote in Romans 3:21-24: "But now a righteousness from God, apart from law, has been made known, to which the Law and the Prophets testify. This righteousness from God comes through faith in Jesus Christ to all who believe. There is no difference, for all have sinned and fall short of the glory of God, and are justified freely by his grace through the redemption that came by Christ Jesus."

Saint Paul, the apostle, wrote about the problem of being imprisoned by pride in following the works of the law. He said that following self-righteousness was like being in prison. "Before this faith came, we were held prisoners by the law, locked up until faith should be revealed. So the law was put in charge to lead us to Christ that we might be justified by faith. Now that faith has come, we are no longer under the supervision of the law" (Galatians 3:23-25).

God disillusioned Saint Paul by moving him from comparison to other people to comparison to God himself. That is why Saint Paul could write: "Here is a trustworthy saying that deserves full acceptance: Christ Jesus came into the world to save sinners — of whom I am the worst" (1 Timothy 1:15).

Comparing Ourselves To God

The tax collector in our story did many things wrong, but he did one thing right. He repented. The illusion under which the tax collector labored was that he was beyond the reach of help. "He stood at a distance" (Luke 18:13a), not thinking himself worthy of coming close to the altar of God. "He would not even look up to heaven" (Luke 18:13b), not thinking himself worthy of even glancing at God. "He beat his breast and said, 'God, have mercy on me, a sinner' " (Luke 18:13b), knowing that he was not deserving of any reward. God disillusioned the tax collector. He justified him by grace, through faith.

The tax collector did not expect to recover from his self-made predicament of being a traitor to the Jews by collecting taxes for Rome and lining his pockets at the expense of the Jewish people. He did not expect that he would receive anything except punishment from God. He was freed from his illusions precisely because he knew that he was unworthy of being saved. The paradox of Christianity in this parable is that it is at the moment that we see that we are unworthy, that God clothes us in righteousness. God saves us by grace.

Justice means getting what you deserve. Mercy means not getting what you deserve. Grace means getting what you do not deserve. This is a parable about grace.

Like alcoholics who bottom out, we only start for home when we truly hit bottom and know it. Luther put it this way, "It is God's nature to create out of nothing. If you are not yet nothing, he won't make anything out of you." Recovery starts only when we know that we are beyond recovery using the system under which we have labored. That we are beyond recovery is an illusion, but we are not freed from that illusion until we believe that we deserve nothing from God.

This parable is an important biblical corrective for our day of ethical relativism. We live in a society where many think that there are no absolutes or, to put it more accurately, many think that the only absolute is that there are no absolutes. Many believe that lying, adultery, promiscuity, and rebelling at all authority are not wrong. The Ten Commandments are not absolutes, many say. Joe Fletcher popularized the philosophy of ethical relativism back in the 1960s. In the early part of the twenty-first century, this philosophy has become the chaotic creed of the majority. Recently I saw a sign on a car that read, "If it feels good, do it." That is an expression of ethical relativism.

Look again at the Pharisee. Look again at the dangers of self-righteousness which leads to the lack of repentance. Look again at the man who felt no guilt, comparing himself favorably to others, instead of God. Look again at the man who exalted himself.

Look again at the tax collector. Look again at his guilt. Look again at his repentance. Look again at his forgiveness. Look again at the man who compared himself to God and saw himself for what he was, an undeserving sinner. Look again at the man who humbled himself before God and was surprised by forgiveness and grace.

No guilt, no grace. Many have tried to make all behavior relative, trying to avoid guilt. Karl Menninger described this problem in his book, *Whatever Became of Sin?* In a more recent book, *The Road Less Travelled*, M. Scott Peck points out that people start down the wide road that leads to destruction precisely because they refuse to take responsibility for their own actions, blaming others instead of acknowledging their own wrong deeds.

Look again, modern man (and woman), and ask, "Whatever will become of my sin?" The parable of the Pharisee and the tax collector is all about illusions about sin. You can either miss the opportunity to take responsibility for your sins and continue to live in the land of illusions, or feel guilt for what you have done wrong, and bring that guilt to the only place where it can be resolved. The cross of Jesus Christ is the place to discover the grace of God and recover from the sins that inhibit you and hold you back from being the full person God intends you to be.

Points To Ponder

1. *Secrets of the heart.* This parable comes alive because Jesus lets us see the secrets in the hearts of the two men in the Temple. Secrets can seduce us.

2. *Luke 18:8b.* The front-side context of our text is about judgment day when the Son of Man will return and find that many people do not really have faith in God.

3. *Luke 18:15-17.* The back-side context of our text is about children who have simple trust in God. Jesus says, "Anyone who does not receive the kingdom of God like a little child will never enter it."

4. *The Pharisee.* Not all Pharisees were self-righteous, but this one is decidedly so. He catalogues his works of the law and looks down on others, including the tax collector who apparently is in the back of the Temple. This Pharisee is filled with pride and prejudice.

5. *The tax collector.* In Jesus' time, tax collectors were Jews who sold out to Rome, not only collecting taxes for the hated conquerors of the Jews, but also lining their pockets in the process. This particular tax collector saw the error of his ways and repented. Jesus taught that anyone can recover from their sins if they repent.

6. *This is a parable about prayer.* See Luke 18:1-8 where the theme is persistent prayer. Here the theme is humble prayer.

7. *Martin Luther radically horizontalized good works.* Good works are to be done for the neighbor, not to get a reward in heaven.

Questions For Personal Consideration
And/Or Group Discussion

1. Read Romans 1:17, Romans 3:23-24, and Romans 5:1.

    How are we justified before God?

2. Read Galatians 2:16 and Galatians 3:24.

    Fill in the blank space in this sentence: We are not justified by doing the works of the law, but by _____ _____.

3. If you are in a group, discuss ethical relativism as you see it in our society today.

4. If you are in a group, consider writing and then enacting a short two-act play on this parable.

See **Digging Deeper**, p. 172, for further insights and applications.

Tips For Small Group Leaders

Below you will find tips for teachers of adult classes and leaders of small study groups that meet at the church or in homes.

1.   Start and/or end each study session with prayer.

2.   Use **Points To Ponder** as a way to examine background and verses of the parables to be studied. You may want to read certain of these **Points To Ponder** to your group in advance of the study session, during the session, or after it. Those members of the group who have their own copies of *Stories To Remember*, should be encouraged to look at the **Points To Ponder** in advance of reading the chapter they are studying.

3.   It is best for all participants to have copies of *Stories To Remember*, but the book is designed so that the leader or teacher can use it as a study guide and the participants can use their Bibles without a copy of *Stories To Remember*. If you choose the latter method, it is cheaper than everyone having a copy of the book, but not better. If you should choose this method, you should order copies of *Stories To Remember* for those participants who desire their own copies.

4.   Use **Questions For Personal Consideration And/Or Group Discussion** as a way to start group discussions or for personal reflection.

5.   As time allows, use **Digging Deeper**, pages 155-172, at the back of this book, for further insights and applications of the parables.

6.   *Stories To Remember* is designed to be used weekly, bi-monthly, or monthly by groups. The study may be divided into two sections of eight chapters each.

7. Try to get members of your group involved in the parables of Jesus, rather than lecturing on the materials in the chapters. Participation means increased understanding and retention.

8. For ways and means to get people involved in group study and insights into small group ministry, one of the most important movements in current church life, read my book, *Way To Grow! Dynamic Church Growth Through Small Groups* (CSS Publishing Company, Lima, Ohio).

Digging Deeper

This section on **Digging Deeper** is intended for your further consideration of each chapter in this book for your devotional life, group study, or class consideration. You are invited to ask, "What difference does each parable make in my life?" As you consider each of the parables this way, two questions will be asked:

1. How does this parable affect your understanding of God? and
2. How does this parable affect your actions for God?

The section on understanding God not only refers to your intellectual comprehension and theology, but to your spirituality as well. The word "understand" literally means "to stand under" something or someone greater than yourself. To stand under the parables of Jesus means that we are open to the possibility of adoration.

About the spiritual experience of adoration, Teilhard de Chardin says:

> *To adore means to lose oneself in the unfathomable, to plunge into the inexhaustible, to find peace in the incorruptible, to be absorbed in defined immensity, to offer oneself to the fire ... and to give one's deepest to that whose depth has no end.*[19]

In a simple, but profound way, a peasant woman described adoration like this: "I look at him and he looks at me."[20] By digging deeper into each parable, we expose ourselves to the possibility of spiritual adoration and examine what it means to look at the Lord and have him look back at us.

The section on action related to the parables will raise questions about how the stories of Jesus can move us to doing something for God and other people. It is one thing to draw closer to God through the stories of Jesus; it is another to be moved to action for the Lord.

The point of departure for this approach comes from the parable of the good Samaritan (Luke 10:25-37). An expert in the law (a Scribe), says to Jesus, "Teacher, what must I do to inherit eternal life?"

Jesus replies, "What is written in the law? How do you read it?"

The Scribe answers, "Love the Lord your God with all your heart and with all your soul and with all your strength and with all your mind" (Deuteronomy 6:5) and "Love your neighbor as yourself" (Leviticus 19:18). The first point of this Scripture called the Great Commandment is to understand, literally to stand under, God. The second part is to put this love into action by loving our neighbors.

While no one can design a program to increase another person's spirituality or action, it is my prayer that this section on **Digging Deeper** may assist you in your growth in loving the Lord and in loving your neighbors. As I wrote this book, I found many areas where the parables of Jesus awakened me in both areas. I hope you, the reader, will make similar discoveries and pay more careful attention to God's Word. Hebrews 2:1 says, "We must pay more careful attention, therefore, to what we have heard, so that we do not drift away."

Chapter One
Six Snapshots
(Matthew 13:31-33, 44-52)

Increasing Your Understanding Of God

1. Do any or all of the six "snapshots" of God's kingdom help you ...
   to see God more clearly?
   to love him more?
   to desire to develop your spirituality further?

2. Do your heart, soul, strength, or mind resonate with any or all of these six "snapshots"?

Increasing Your Actions For God

1. Are you planting small bits of leaven in other people's lives?

2. What are the financial implications of any of these parables?

3. How can we maintain the truths about God as revealed in the Bible, yet refrain from quick or false judgments about the uncommitted or superficially committed people we know?

4. How can we retain the best of Christian traditions and yet be open to changes that need to be made?

Chapter Two
Six Questions
(Luke 10:25-37)

Increasing Your Understanding Of God

1. In what ways does this parable cause you to want to love the Lord more?

2. Does this parable offer any help for your personal devotions?

Increasing Your Actions For God

1. As a result of a Bible study on this parable, one church started a "Go And Do Likewise" ministry of painting houses, trimming trees, and doing other fix-up work free for neighborhood widows and other needy people. Would something like this work in your church?

2. How can you be a good Samaritan at home and at work?

Chapter Three
Ready Or Not, Here I Come
(Luke 12:13-21, 40)

Increasing Your Understanding Of God

1. What do you understand the Bible to teach about "being rich toward God" (Luke 12:21)?

2. Read 2 Timothy 3:1-5 and write down your paraphrase of these verses here.

    _____

    _____

    If you are in a group, discuss the paraphrases of the members of the group.

3. Read 1 Corinthians 15:51-57. What does this passage say about death?

4. Philippians 2:10-11 says that the day is coming when "at the name of Jesus every knee should bow, in heaven and in earth, and every tongue confess that Jesus Christ is Lord, to the glory of God the Father." What does that mean?

Increasing Your Actions For God

1. What can you do to get ready for meeting God at the time of death?

2. Read 2 Timothy 4:1-8. What do these verses have to do with helping others prepare to meet God?

Chapter Four
Four Warnings
(Luke 13:18-30)

Increasing Your Understanding Of God

1. Read Hebrews 2:1 and write down some ways we must pay careful attention to what we have heard in theses four warnings in Luke 13.

2. In what ways do these four warnings help you focus on your relationship with God?

Increasing Your Actions For God

1. Re-read Hebrews 2:1. Write down ways by which you can help others pay attention to the four warnings of Luke 13.

2. Read Acts 23:6-15. Paul was in custody for being a Christian witness. If you were arrested for being a Christian, what evidence would there be against you?

Chapter Five
Party Humility And Hospitality
(Luke 14:1, 7-14)

Increasing Your Understanding Of God

1. How does the parable about humility and hospitality relate to you and your adoration of God?

2. In Celtic spirituality there is a *5 P* exercise that can help us today. Try it.
   a. *Pause*. Stop what you are doing. Let yourself relax. Let all tension out of your body. Make space for God.
   b. *Presence*. Know that God is with you as he promised to be. Pray that God will be present with you as you think about all that he has done for you.
   c. *Picture*. In your mind's eye, see Jesus on the cross. Listen to his words.
   d. *Ponder*. Consider what these words mean as they are spoken to you.
   e. *Promise*. Tell God that you will come back into his presence again and again.

Increasing Your Actions For God

1. In what ways does the parable about humility and hospitality encourage you to act toward your neighbor?

2. Would you consider throwing a party for the needy at church or in your home with no view of repayment? How would you organize this kind of party? Who would help?

3. In what other ways can you put the parable into action?

Chapter Six
RSVP: Avoiding Attractive Distractions
(Luke 14:15-24)

Increasing Your Understanding Of God

1. What experiences have you had that have encouraged you to think of God only as a judge and Christianity as a religion of duty, gloom, and doom?

2. Celtic spirituality teaches that we can have a sense of the joyful presence of God even in times of adversity by using what the Celts called the *Caim*, the Encircling. Using a stick or a finger, the ancient Christian Celts would encircle their heads and invoke the presence of the Holy Trinity. The circle was said to accompany the believer on his journey through life. It was viewed as a reminder of Jesus' promise to be present with us even in danger.

   Try it as a way to rise above your circumstances and avoid the attractive distractions of life.

3. Prayer: Lord, we did not hear you when you were hungry or thirsty. Lord, we did not see you when you were a stranger, or needed clothes. Lord, we did not visit you when you were sick or in prison. Lord, you came to us again and again and we frequently missed you. Forgive us, Lord.

Increasing Your Actions For God

1. Name someone who has loved you in the past by filling in the blanks below.

   _____ loved me by _____.

2. Then scratch out the name you marked down and replace it with the name of Jesus.

3. Then promise to put the exercise into practice by loving someone else this week like you have been loved.

Chapter Seven
The Wonderful Party And The Strange Guests
(Luke 14:15-24)

Increasing Your Understanding Of God

1. Read Ephesians 2:8-10. If you are a part of a group, discuss these verses. What difference do these verses make in your relationship with God?

2. Read Luke 10:25-37. These verses contain what is called the Great Commandment to love the Lord your God with all your heart, soul, strength, and mind. Why do you love God so much?

3. When you consider God's love and grace and look at him, you discover that he has been looking at you all of your life. What difference does that make?

Increasing Your Actions For God

1. In the light of this parable, what is evangelism? Is it recruitment for church membership?

2. Do the "bums in the bushes" include alcoholics and drug addicts?

3. What does timing have to do with reaching people for Christ?

Chapter Eight
Wake Up!
(Matthew 25:14-30)

Increasing Your Understanding Of God

1. God is generous, so generous, in fact, that he gives us salvation free of charge. Salvation is free, but it is not without cost. Who pays that cost?

2. How is that cost paid?

3. What difference does this make in your relationship with God?

Increasing Your Actions For God

1. Since God is so generous, shouldn't we be generous givers? Gratefulness and joyous generosity are at the heart of Christian stewardship. If you are in a group, discuss this concept.

2. What do the words of Mother Teresa of Calcutta, "Doing something beautiful for God," mean?

3. If you have never taken a "Spiritual Gifts Inventory," request one from your pastor or your church. This inventory will help you discover your spiritual gifts.

Chapter Nine
Punctured Misconceptions
About The Lost And Found
(Luke 15:1-32)

Increasing Your Understanding Of God

1. What misconceptions of God are punctured by Jesus in Luke 15?

2. In the Old Testament we read that the people were severely punished for murmuring against God and Moses in the wilderness. Why does God hate murmuring so much?

3. Prayer: Lord, forgive me for the times when I am sucked into the cesspool of murmuring against you or other people. Chaos is catching and I too easily succumb. Forgive me. In Jesus' name. Amen.

Increasing Your Actions For God

Since in Luke 15 Jesus invites us to be more like God in our actions, consider these promises to God:

1. I promise to refrain from murmuring against other people because I know how much it hurts you when I murmur.

2. In spite of the probable consequences of unpopularity, I will speak up for those whom others tear down.

Chapter Ten
The Predicament Of The Loving Father
(Luke 15:11-32)

Increasing Your Understanding Of God

In Luke 15:11-32 Jesus invites us to see what God is like.

1. How does the understanding of the God of grace affect your devotional life?

2. How does the understanding of the God of grace affect your church life?

3. How does the understanding of the God of grace affect your everyday life?

Increasing Your Actions For God

1. In our personal lives we, like the heavenly Father, are caught in the predicament between the need for justice and the tug of grace. Describe some of the conflicts that arise because of this predicament.

2. One of the long-standing battles in the Christian life is the tension between the Law and the Gospel. How does this tension show up in government? In the justice system? In the organized church? At work?

3. Consider the nature of witnessing to our faith in the light of the return home to the Father by appropriating what Christ has accomplished on the cross.

Chapter Eleven
The Predicament Of The Elder Son
(Luke 15:1-2, 11-32)

Increasing Your Understanding Of God

1. A psychiatrist once said about one of his patients, "Edythe is bound on the north, the south, the east, and the west by Edythe." What does this mean in relationship to God?

2. Another psychiatrist described one of his patients like this: "Sally is a faded, jaded narcissist." What problem does Sally have with God?

3. Discuss the statement: "Cultural Christianity is different than relational faith."

Increasing Your Actions For God

1. Discuss this question: "If we are saved by grace through faith in Jesus Christ and not by good works" (Ephesians 2:8-9), what does this mean for evangelical outreach to those who do not believe in Jesus Christ?"

2. Discuss this question: "If evangelism means assisting people to find maturity in Christ" (Colossians 1:28), how does that change your actions toward those who do not have a relationship with Christ?"

Chapter Twelve
Who Could Ask For Anything More?
(Matthew 19:27-30; 20:1-16)

Increasing Your Understanding Of God

1. Pray the prayer many Christians pray before coming to Holy Communion:
    "We do not presume to come to this your table, O merciful Lord, trusting in our own righteousness, but in your manifold and great mercies. We are not worthy so much as to gather up the crumbs under your table. But you are the same Lord whose mercy is unfailing."

2. What can be learned about the amazing grace of God in this parable?

3. Consider again the words about stories by Marty Haugen at the beginning of this chapter.

4. What does the title of this chapter mean?

Increasing Your Actions For God

1. What should our attitude toward latecomers to faith be?

2. Why is there so much envy, jealousy, and complaining in the church as well as in the world?

3. What "Aha moments" did you experience as you considered this parable?

4. Consider the three laws of the Christian life in **Points To Ponder**.

Chapter Thirteen
A Puzzling Parable With A Sharp Point
(Luke 16:1-15)

Increasing Your Understanding Of God

1. Consider this statement: "Christian stewardship has to do with the love of God." If you are in a group, discuss the statement.

2. The Gospel we hear each Sunday in church may pass over our heads without touching our minds or our hearts. If you are in a small group, break into groups of two. Put your hands on your partner's head and say these words:

   The Lord bless you and keep you.
   The Lord make his face shine on you and be gracious
       to you.
   The Lord look upon you with favor and give you peace.

   Then make the sign of the cross on your partner's forehead as a reminder of baptism.

3. Reverse roles.

Increasing Your Actions For God

1. Consider this statement and develop an action plan based on it: "Christian stewardship has to do with love of my neighbor." If you are in a group, share your plan with your partner and listen to his or her action plan. Phone one another within the week to check on how you are doing with your plan.

2. Secretly, use money for some needy person(s) this week. Take no credit for what you do.

Chapter Fourteen
The Man Who Never Noticed
(Luke 16:19-31)

Increasing Your Understanding Of God

1. You might try this prayer as a way to draw closer to God:
   Dear Father, we are not all we should be. We have not done all we should have done in your name. At times we have ignored people or been insensitive to the needy or not seen people who cross our paths because we are too busy. At times we have hurt you by not paying attention to them. Forgive us, we pray, and help us to be more sensitive to those whom you place in our pathways in life. In Jesus' name. Amen.

2. Which of the Ten Commandments relate to loving God?

Increasing Your Actions For God

1. Do something good in secret for someone this week. Don't tell the recipient who did the good deed. Don't tell anyone what you have done. Do your deed in the name of Jesus.

2. Consider Jesus' three temptations in Matthew 4:1-11. If you are in a group, discuss this passage.

3. Consider Matthew 25:31-46. If you are in a group, discuss this passage.

4. Which of the Ten Commandments relate to loving your neighbor?

Chapter Fifteen
The Pushy Widow
(Luke 18:1-8)

Increasing Your Understanding Of God

1. Are there times when a Christian should be indomitable with God?

2. How far is too far in relationship to being pushy with God?

3. What does the coming of the Son of Man mean for our relationship with God?

4. Prayer: Lord, teach us the times to push on, even when we are discouraged with our prayer lives and you don't seem to be listening. In these dark nights of the soul, help us to keep on keeping on. In Jesus' name. Amen.

Increasing Your Actions For God

1. Are there times when a Christian should be indomitable with his or her neighbor?

2. How far is too far in being pushy with our neighbors?

3. What does the coming of the Son of Man mean for our witnessing to our neighbors?

4. Prayer: Lord, teach us to be sensitive to our neighbors, knowing when to say the right words in the right ways at the right times to the glory of your name. In Jesus' name. Amen.

Chapter Sixteen
The Recovery Of Guilt And Grace
(Luke 18:9-14)

Increasing Your Understanding Of God

1. What illusions do people have about God?

2. What illusions do people have about what God expects from us?

3. What illusions do people have about forgiveness?

4. Prayer: Lord, we are not worthy to receive any good from your hands. We deserve only punishment for what we have thought, our word, and our deeds. We have left much undone that we should have done. We are totally dependent on your grace in Jesus Christ. In Jesus' holy name we humbly come before your throne of grace. Amen.

Increasing Your Actions For God

1. What illusions do people have about themselves?

2. What illusions do people have about other people?

3. If you are in a group studying this parable, discuss this statement: "Luther radically horizontalized good works."

Endnotes

Chapter Four
1. Carl Braaten, *Church Dogmatics*, "The Historical Jesus and the King-dom of God" (Philadelphia: Fortress, 1984), p. 483.

2. Leslie Newbiggen, *Sign of the Kingdom* (Grand Rapids, MI: Eerdman's, 1981), p. 37.

3. Tony Campolo, *The Kingdom of God Is a Party* (Word Publishing Co, 1990), pp. 27-28.

Chapter Five
4. Max Lucado, *And the Angels Were Silent* (Portland: Multnomah, 1992), p. 142.

Chapter Six
5. William Barclay, *Commentary on Luke* (Philadelphia: Westminster Press, 1975), pp. 102-103.

Chapter Ten
6. Helmut Thielicke, *The Waiting Father* (New York: Harper and Broth-ers, 1959), pp. 17-18.

7. Wes Seelinger, "Semi-Prodigals" in *Faith At Work* magazine, June, 1973, p. 11.

Chapter Eleven
8. William Barclay, *The Gospel of Luke* (Philadelphia: Westminster Press, 1975), p. 204.

Chapter Twelve
9. Marty Haugen, "The Song of Mark," cassette tape (Chicago: GIA Publications, 1995).

10. Eugene Lowry, *How to Preach a Parable* (Nashville: Abingdon Press, 1990), p. 124. Lowry is the preacher who put me on to the title of this chapter.

11. *Ibid.*, p. 128.

12. Song "Borning Cry" by John Ylvisaker.

13. William Barclay, *The Gospel of Matthew* (Philadelphia: Westminster Press, 1975), pp. 220-222.

Chapter Thirteen
14. Lowry, *op. cit.*, p. 33.

15. Thielicke, *op. cit,.* p. 102.

Chapter Fifteen
16. William Barclay, *The Gospel of Luke*, *op. cit.*, p. 222.

17. *Interpreter's Bible*, Volume VIII (New York/Nashville: Abingdon/ Cokesbury Press, 1952), p. 307.

18. William Barclay, *The Gospel of Luke*, *op. cit.*, p. 222.

Digging Deeper
19. Teilhard de Chardin, *Le Milieu Divin* (Collins Fontana, 1975), p. 127.

20. David Adam, *The Open Gate* (Triangle, SPCK, 1994), p. 38.

Postscript

As a senior seminarian, I was fascinated by a book on the parables of Jesus called *The Waiting Father*. It was written by Helmut Thielicke. Over forty years of ministry, I have picked up that book and found value there on many occasions. The parables of Jesus often inspire me, sometimes confuse me, and always challenge me. *The Waiting Father* has always been there as a resource to which I can return. I hope my book, *Stories To Remember*, will be of some help for a searcher for God. Perhaps a preacher or teacher of God's Word, a student or, a small group participant will find *Stories To Remember* helpful in understanding the greatness and wonder of our God. In addition, I hope this book will help someone do what Mother Teresa calls "doing something beautiful for God." The stories of Jesus are powerful.

The importance of stories became clear to me when I became a Christian in 1957. Stories, especially the stories of Jesus, give us space for grace. When I first got in touch with Hebrew thinking, I was amazed to see how this system of thinking is grounded in stories. Not definitions, but illustrations — that is what Hebrew thinking is all about.

The importance of stories to convey biblical thought patterns came to the forefront of my mind again when I studied Celtic Christianity in England and Ireland in 1997. Celtic Christians passed on the great truths of the Lord by telling stories.

It is my hope that *Stories To Remember* will help you, the reader, better to stand, with head bowed, under the master storyteller of all time, Jesus Christ, our Lord.